SUMMER IN BROOKLYN

1969-1975

SUMMER IN BROOKLYN

1969-1975

RICHARD GRAYSON

Superstition Mountain Press

Phoenix – 2008

Printed in the United States of America.

Superstition Mountain Press
4303 E. Cactus Road
Phoenix, AZ 85032

First Edition

ISBN 978-0-6152-3794-7

10 9 8 7 6 5 4 3 2 1

For Jonathan Baumbach

Summer in Brooklyn

1969-1975

Monday, May 26, 1975

A kind of manic Memorial Day. This morning I drove
into Manhattan & went to the old U.S. Customs
House (a magnificent building) to the Second N.Y.
Book Fair. Last summer I went to the first one, at the
Cultural Center on Columbus Circle - that place
owned by Huntington Hartford.

All the small presses & little magazines & various
feminist, Third World, gay & radical publications had
set up exhibits, just like last year's. It was a kind of
huge candy store for me, going from table to table
collecting leaflets & catalogues, & looking somewhat
wistfully at all the books, pamphlets & magazines I
could not afford to buy, & signing up for mailing lists.

At the table for The Magazines - 6 fairly well-known
publications including *Fiction* (published by Mark
Mirsky at CCNY - his new novel just came out,
published by the Fiction Collective) & *Partisan Review*,
I saw a somewhat familiar figure with a *Parnassus*
head visor. I asked him if he was Herb Leibowitz &
he said yes & I told him I was Richard Grayson. He
said he enjoyed many parts of my thesis, particularly
"The Peacock Room." I thanked him for the kind

words & told him I'd drop off the other copy of my thesis at his office so I can get my M.A. this summer. He said they're having a meeting of the M.A. Committee on Wednesday, & they're probably going to eliminate the comprehensive exam. I told him I was teaching at LIU & said I'd see him around. He's the editor of *Parnassus - Poetry in Review* & a frequent book reviewer for the Sunday Times.

The Fiction Collective had a table, but the coordinator of it, Peggy Humphreys, would be there on Wednesday. Moving from table to table, I felt surrounded by kindred spirits: poets, fiction writers, literary people. (It probably was a great place to get laid; various black-stockinged girls with granny glasses & long dresses were similarly moseying along.)

I came across the *New Writers* table & introduced myself to the editors, Connie Glickman & Miriam Easton (both pleasant, Jewish & 40ish), whom I've corresponded with. They showed me Volume 2, Number 3 of *New Writers* with my story in it; I decided to buy a couple of copies even tho they said they'd just mailed my contributor's copies out to me. They said I should send them another manuscript. It felt surprisingly good to see my name & "Rampant Burping" in print; I was more than a little excited, & when I came home, Mom & Dad made a semi-big fuss over the magazine.

Lest I should get a big head, however, I ran into an editor from a little magazine who had rejected "Alice Keppel." I didn't say who I was, but got to talking to him, & he said he always sent criticism except when rejecting manuscripts of no value whatsoever. Needless to say, I got my story returned that way, without even a note.

But I feel at home in the semi-underground, somewhat counterculture literary world. I see it's much easier to publish poetry than fiction & much easier if you're a woman (& probably easier still if you're a lesbian).

Alice, my own friendly neighborhood little publisher, came over this afternoon after finishing the latest issue of *Henrietta*. We had a raucous time, for Alice is still the best raconteuse money can't buy; even Mom & Dad think Alice is a genuine original, a kook.

We watched "Another World" (Steve Frame was killed in a copter crash today; the actor playing him had demanded better scripts & was summarily fired) & took a test in the issue of *Cosmopolitan* that Alice brought over, to see what kind of lover we are. (Apparently I'm a manic lover, Alice an eros type.) Alice saw Mr. Blumstein yesterday at the Washington Square art show - she's so crazy about him - & then went to meet Andreas. Alice says I must see the apartment (she still calls it "Renee's place" for lack of a better name): they've painted a fake fireplace on the wall, with a cat sitting on top of it.

Wednesday, May 27, 1970

A cool, gloriously sunny day. This morning I was on my way to the college when I noticed Kjell on his porch. He invited me up & we talked for a couple of hours - we have a lot to talk about. We are both nervous - he has tranquilizers, too. Kjell converted to Judaism recently since is going to marry his girlfriend Sharon. He also signed up for the Reserves. Mrs. W came out on the porch & talked with us for a while - she's such a nice person. I like the Ws - they're fabulous people.

It was so late I decided to grab a bite at home, then I left for school. Mark wasn't around, but Juan & DB on the Spigot staff were in the office. DB & I talked away for hours - he's interested in some of the same things I am: television, modern literature, journalism, playwriting & politics. Another nice person. What's wrong with the word "nice"?

I spoke to both Uncle Marty & Aunt Arlyne. They took Joey home this morning. He's fighting Arlyne & refuses to open his eye, but is fine. Everyone's tired from the tension of the last few days.

On the bus going home I talked with Mrs. J & I tried to impress her. I want people to think I'm fantastic.

Tonight, with a story about Brad swimming thru my head, I drove to Ave. U & bought the Voice. People make life worthwhile - for me at least - & today was good.

Tuesday, May 28, 1974

It's a cool, sunny afternoon. In a couple of hours I'll take my final in Bogen's class & then all my schoolwork for the term will be done. I got very ambitious at about 11 PM last night, took my typewriter downstairs & knocked off the last paper for Cooley in a couple of hours. So I went to sleep late, had delicious dreams all night & woke up feeling like a new man.

I met Avis at the Junction at noon - she's very involved with finals until next week. But she mentioned that she went to the ballet with Teresa on Sunday & they want to do something with me before they each leave town. I went to LaG to hang out for awhile before heading downtown. Mike is staying in the student government office until June 30, when the fiscal year ends. Eddie was around, trying not to look to anxious about him & Rose moving in.

I enjoyed hanging out with Ross & Susan, & I cuddled a little with Libby (everyone touches her & she's always kissing people). Debbie said that they're having a party next week & that Ronna & I are invited, while Laila said she'll be around this summer

& that I should call her & we'll go out on her cabin
cruiser. It was especially good to see Vito - I miss him
a lot. We discussed movies & other junk, just like old
times. Then I went to my session with Mrs. Ehrlich.

I discussed my dream about having a surprise
birthday. She felt it was curious it that I had had it on
the weekend of my parents' silver wedding
anniversary; I didn't have a party for them because I
didn't want to go through all the trouble. But then I
realized that I've never given a party. Part of the
reason is because I'm afraid of a failure, but Mrs. E
feels that more importantly, I worry about being
"sucked dry." It's a term she's used in connection with
sex, too.

What she means is I'm afraid to give of myself, my
vital essences, freely. I suppose it ties in with my
childhood fear of vomiting. It may even have
something to do with the difficulty I've been having
lately coming to orgasm. I have no trouble getting
erections, but in sex play, it takes me such a long time
to come & sometimes I don't. Yet though I don't give
of myself, I do put myself out for other people,
always with the hope that they'll reciprocate. Which is
probably why I always remember everybody's
birthdays & I'm disappointed every year when I don't
hear from everyone.

Mrs. E liked the way I put it when I said was "an
accountant of the emotions," keeping mental books on

how much love or stroking I've given to this or that person & what they've given me in return. I need material approval from a lot of people because I have this underlying sense of worthlessness - so what if I've made Phi Beta Kappa? And it's especially on my mind now when I'm preparing to seek employment. I'm putting myself on the open market to be evaluated; potential employers can say what I'm worth. And, as Mrs. E said, reality is that it will be difficult because these are rough economic times & jobs are scarce.

And I discussed with Mrs. E a dream I had last night: there was a reunion of my friends from public school & junior high. It was triggered by seeing my old pal & fellow member of the Sultans, Arnie, in Kings Plaza yesterday. Part of the reason I didn't go over to him was because I wanted him to come over to me first. I am pretty anxious, but this summer will prove interesting. I'm putting myself to a test of my manhood, I suppose. Although maybe I shouldn't look at it that way...

Tuesday, May 29, 1973

I've been moody these past couple of days. I have my English final tomorrow afternoon & my Afro-American Lit final on Monday, & I have hardly studied for either. To tell you the truth, I don't care *what* I get on these tests. I feel as if I'd like to be *out* of school already & over with the whole damn thing.

I guess it's just that the glamorous part of graduating is over - except, that is, for commencement - & now it's reality time, which is usually a letdown. Which means (after finals): finding a summer job, deciding definitely on a grad school, getting an apartment, leaving my friends. I am going to resent having to become an adult, but like the man says, it's got to be done.

I've really had it easy these past few years: no job, no responsibilities except schoolwork, nothing to do but hang around & explore life with people. There's so much drudgery in life, that either thru my upbringing or inclinations, I can't accept. I want to be an artist, an observer - all right, a rich effete snob, if you will.

They call it "getting into the world." Well, I take a look at this world we have & I want to puke - there's so much ugliness & pain. Which is why I'm taking refuge in the study of literature (oh yes, I *understand* my motive) - a world of beauty, elegance, & when the ugliness & pain are present, at least they're depicted beautifully.

I went to LaG today. Brenda said she saw me on the TV show; I'm liking her more & more. Tony was in his usual top form, & Susan said she & Felicia were definitely going to Europe - it must be a relief to Ronna that she's not 'ruining' Susan's summer.

Vito & I reminisced about her our first meeting, almost exactly a year ago, & Mikey agreed with me that he was fed up with finals, too. I talked with Debbie & Bruce & B.J. & Avis - I'm going to miss those little time-wasting talks more than anything else at college. I tried to study this afternoon, but I got disgusted & so, to cheer myself up, I had my hair styled at Cutting Crib.

Tuesday, May 30, 1972

A warm, humid day. The car was having new gears put in today, so Mom drove me to school. I paid my consolidated fee of $51.50 for both summer sessions & went to Roosevelt to register. I'm taking only one English course first session - Modern Drama with Prof. Galin. The second I'm going to take Classics 1 again & a Poli Sci course on race. Coming out of the gym, I met Gary, who finished registering, & Timmy, who was about to institute "emergency Plan A" to avoid getting closed out.

Back at LaG, I found B.J. & Libby, Mike & Mikey, & Elspeth. It looks as tho a lot of people will be around this summer; Elayne & Charles will be taking courses, too. Mikey told me that Ira was hit by a car while riding his bicycle yesterday - he hurt his knee badly & required 18 stitches. I was really upset, but tonight I called Ira & he said he was okay, he'd just have to stay off his leg for a week, but his bike was wrecked.

I had lunch with Mikey, Mike, Ari, B.J. & Libby, & Moe, who'll be leaving for British Columbia next week. Mikey thinks his chances of going to Miami as a delegate are diminished now that the regular slate, heretofore "uncommitted," is also backing McGovern. Mike seemed back to normal again, probing everyone's emotions.

After lunch, I went with Mikey & Mike as they got permission to get into an Anthro elective, then sat down next to Stacy on the grass. She was friendly (with *another* "I was going to call you") & we talked until a sunshower came & we had to go inside. Stacy will forever be an enigma to me.

I went out for some tea with Ronna & Susan; Ronna & I are getting quite close for the first time, & I think she's learning to trust me. I can see how much her parents' divorce has hurt her.

I left to take a taxi to Dr. Wouk. B.J. & everyone else say I don't need therapy, that I'm healthier than anyone in LaG, but I want to stay healthy & today we had a good session. Dr. Wouk thinks I should sleep with Avis, that she wants me to - but I'm not sure he's right.

Tonight I called Marty & Rose. She's still weak but better & he's enjoying teaching most of the time but doesn't want to make it a career.

Monday, May 31, 1971

Another cloudy, rainy, miserable day. May ended today with Memorial Day. Tomorrow is the first of June, & five months of 1971 have whizzed by. At the start of this year I would have never guessed what things have happened, especially my romance with Shelli. By the end of the week I shall be twenty years old, two decades of living. Yet I feel I've only begun to live. I didn't really begin living until perhaps two years ago, when I started to recover. Despite the fact that my bar mitzvah was 7 years ago, I have just recently become a man.

I had a dream-racked sleep last night. I hurried to Kings Plaza after breakfast to take advantage of the sales in the department store. But the place was already a madhouse, with women fighting each other for bargains & hundreds of people milling about, trying to get something for nothing. I got disgusted & walked to the Pants Set, which was empty - Cousin Merryl was in the store. I came home, watched some soap operas & went to pick up Shelli.

We took a long drive in the drizzly weather to Coney Island. This was the first day the beach & the amusements opened, but Shelli didn't really want to stop, & I wasn't too enthusiastic, either - Coney Island, is sad to say, a bad slum. We got onto the Belt, & as Shelli wanted to visit Ivan, I drove to Rockaway. But Ivan wasn't home, so we headed back to

Brooklyn, fighting the Kings Plaza traffic. We bought Italian ices on Utica Ave. & went to my house. In my bedroom, we had a good time, laughing & frolicking (Mike says we're always frolicking) & making love (I bought some condoms earlier).

Shelli had to get home early, to prepare for her sister's graduation tomorrow. I'm looking forward to hearing Ramsey Clark. I spoke to Shelli tonight, but she's not feeling well - I hope everything goes all right. On the news, I spotted Mansarde on a film clip of a Madison peace march. Dad took Mom out for their 22nd anniversary tonight. I watched TV, began *Pere Goriot* & prepared to go to bed early.

Monday, June 1, 1970

A bright, humid first of June. Dad could hardly move this morning & stayed home the whole day. Mom took him to Dr. Robbins, the chiropractor, who gave him some treatments. They told Dr. Robbins of my yoga & he heartily approved. I had to take a cab to Dr. Wouk, as the IRT service was delayed. His back hurts him too - he told me he'll be away for August. We discussed my major - he advises me to major in Political Science & minor in English, with an eye towards law school, which leaves a lot of room for me. Dr. Wouk thinks I'll probably end up as a well-adjusted bisexual - but he isn't pressuring me to make a decision about my sexual life right away. There's no hurry, so why not let it be? I stopped in the Slack Bar

& said hello to Grandpa & Joe.

At home I read by the pool for a bit, then bought a pair of tennis sneakers in the shoestore where Stan works. Marc had his braces put back on, & he's been grouchy ever since. Miss Glikin, the bastard, only gave me a B in English. After dinner, I cleaned out my drawers & threw out a lot of junk. I gathered $3 in pennies & gave them to Grandpa Herb. Tonight I went for a hair styling at Joe Pepitone's. Tommy introduced me to Joe Pepitone. I didn't like him - too cocky. Lennie gave me a pretty good haircut, altho I don't like my hair over my ears because it makes me look like a sheepdog. It's been too hot to sleep well.

Saturday, June 2, 1973

A warm evening. I'm going to Scott's party tonight, altho I doubt I will enjoy myself there. I don't really enjoy these huge, see-how-many-friends-I-have affairs, the kind Allan was so fond of. But maybe I'm just jealous because I don't have the nerve to give one & find out how many friends I *really* have. Anyway, I'll go pick up Ronna, & then take Avis - she called to ask if she could hitch a ride with us; I suppose Rob is climbing some mountain in New Paltz or someplace. I have to show up tonight, or else Scott's feelings will be hurt, altho I have to admit that his ego bruises quite easily on matters like these. There will be drinking & smoking, & making out (altho that's kind of déclassé) & little witticisms exchanged between people who see each other every day anyway.

Last evening I went over with Dad to see his parents. Grandma Sylvia is going for her third acupuncture treatment tonight, she misses Miami, & Grandpa Nat looks very tired. I spoke to Gary, too - he's getting out of the depression over his grandfather's death. Gary's mother ended her sitting shiva, & things are getting back to normal there. I got a birthday card from Gary today - he signed Wendy's name to it, too, of course. Other cards (both graduation & birthday) came from Uncle Monty & Aunt Sydelle; Marty, Arlyne & the kids; & Grandpa Herb & Grandma Ethel.

This morning I shopped in Kings Plaza until noon, when I went over to see Ronna - I handed Ronna's sister *her* birthday card. Ronna & I drove into the city, to the Theatre District. We had lunch at Sam & Ben's, where I'd previously taken Donna when we saw "Lysistrata," & also Alice. Then we had tickets for a preview showing of "Uncle Vanya" at the Circle in the Square Theatre. Chekhov's plays still hold up very well, & George C. Scott, Julie Christie, Elizabeth Wilson, Nicol Williamson, Cathleen Nesbit & Lillian Gish were all superb. We met Maddy there with her friend Helene. On the way home, I showed Ronna where she'll be working.

Monday, June 3, 1974

11 PM. In an hour it will be my birthday. Today was pretty good; for one thing, the sun came out, reviving hopes that summer may actually come this year after all. I woke up early this morning & took the subway into Manhattan like any commuter. As I approached Fifth Avenue, I noticed a lot of people outside on the street - the strike was on. The shop steward from the union came up to take Juan off the job - he was reluctant to go - & they wouldn't let anyone ship their goods. Dad says if the strike goes on for a long time, a lot of businesses could go under. He didn't mention anything about Art Pants, but I was afraid to ask him. Business hasn't been very good lately anyway.

For four and a half hours, I did the billing & some bookkeeping; I mailed some letters, made out a deposit slip and took it to the bank with some checks. Dad had to show me what to do, but it wasn't difficult to learn. I had a raging dull headache, probably sinus caused by the weather - Dad was suffering with it also. We had lunch in Brownie's. I left "the place" around 2 PM, feeling that I'd given Dad a bit of a hand (otherwise he would have had to come in on Saturday) & glad to have the $20 he put in my pocket. When I came home from the city, I changed into shorts right away & went to sit in the backyard. Marc & Fern came out to set up the pool for the summer, & I added my strength to help them take the canvas off.

Josh called to ask if he could have the extra ticket to graduation that I've got. Usually I enjoy Josh's cynicism and rebelliousness, but today it was just a bore. He won't wear a gown to graduation, wants to sit in the lily pond during the exercises (exasperated, I tried to explain why he couldn't), is going to be stoned the whole time & doesn't give a flying fuck about studying for finals. He's so anti-establishment, he's almost a caricature. Vito said last week: "Your friend Josh. Oh yes, he's the guy who's so smart he always gets C's." For a while tonight, I just wanted to shake Josh. To top things off, he said he was going to drop by to pick up the ticket & didn't show. He kept talking about his seeing Aurora again & how maybe she would get back together with him (she's dropping out of FIT & is working as a photographer's assistant), but when I mentioned to Josh that I'd passed my comprehensive exam, he didn't seem to hear.

Ronna later said that Josh says "fuck it" to so many things because deep down he's afraid to face their importance; if he does not try at school, he can't fail because of his unwillingness to put himself to the test. I suppose Ronna's right - she's become a rather astute psychologist. Our phone conversation tonight was interrupted a zillion times by the dog barking at her cousin Barbara, by her baby brother's antics, by our going outside (separately) to look at a magnificent red sunset. Ronna's final final is tomorrow, & perhaps I'll see her after her group in the evening. I told her how old I'm getting, that I'm old enough to be her baby brother's father (altho it seems illogical to say that now since I've always known that) & she said she was old enough to be his mother. Her cousin then asked Ronna when she had her first period. Ronna said she was 12, and her cousin replied: "But was Ivan that fast?" I laughed & told Ronna that's what she got for hanging out with 11-year-olds when a sexy guy of 14 like me was available. (I don't think I thought I could do anything with my cock at that age.) Philip Roth's new novel is entitled *My Life as a Man*. I wonder if I've begun mine yet.

Friday, June 4, 1971

My twentieth birthday, a hot & humid day. My eyes & head hurt very much after a good night's sleep. I have congestion in my sinuses & felt dizzy & headachy all day, but I tried not to let it spoil my birthday. Since I felt ill, Shelli said she'd come over here. Mom left me $25 as a gift from her & Dad. I went outside in the backyard, sunning myself by the pool. Shelli came outside & gave me a kiss & my present, a beautiful skinny rib knit shirt in several colors. Her card was beautiful:

A rainy night in Prospect Park
I realized I loved you
I'd never loved anyone as I loved you then
I love you more now

We talked quietly in the yard in the hot sun as we got

very tan. After lunch we went to Kings Plaza, where I wanted to spend my birthday money. I saw my stepcousin Merryl in the store - she's going to teaching riding at camp this summer. I bought jasmine tea, fluffy white socks & at Macy's, a beautiful small gold peace sign on a gold chain like the one Shelli's cousin's boyfriend has. Shelli & I went for coffee in The Apple Tree - we didn't say very much, but then we don't have to. She was having trouble with her period, so at home we just kissed & fooled around, which was enjoyable enough.

I got a lot of birthday cards: sentimental ones from my grandparents; funny ones from Mom & Dad & my brothers & Gary; a cute one from Alice; & a surprise, a card from Brad that read, "I wish we were together... hand in hand...arm in arm..." Shelli must have wondered why a guy would send me a card like that, but I think she understood. I'm going to call Brad. Is it possible that he's been in love with me still all these years? Shelli & I took a long drive tonight after dinner, smiling & laughing & making each other happy. When I kissed her goodnight, I realize that I never thought I'd ever be this happy. I stopped at Irving Cohen's house, where his wife gave me a birthday kiss, & then at home the family had a birthday cake waiting. You know something? I'm the luckiest man alive.

Thursday, June 5, 1975

10 PM. I'm just 'coming down' from having written since early afternoon. I completed a story called "In the Lehman Collection," without Mao, but it's very much like "Garibaldi." I got very worn out after writing, even with these pieces that aren't taken from my own private life. It's as if the skin were torn away, & I were a mass of bones & nerve endings. But it's wonderful to know that I can write without the constant pressure of the MFA program; I *feel* like a writer now, or at least an apprentice writer.

At least I'm good at creative writing because so far I'm a washout at creative dreaming. The last two nights I've not been able to stop myself from being frustrated. In the first dream, two nights ago, I was taking Prof. Heffernan's final & stepped out of the room to get a drink of water; when I returned, she was leaving with the exams because the test was over. Frantic, I returned to my desk, but it was cluttered with papers & I couldn't find my final. Last night's dream was also set in a classroom: I was trying to take down an important announcement, but couldn't do it because of continual interruptions. I tried to follow the book's advice & take positive action, but it's didn't work & both times I awoke feeling terribly frustrated. I've had dreams along these lines for years. I did have a dream in which Harvey appeared & was quite nasty & sneaky, so unlike the picture I have of him.

Perhaps I dreamed of Harvey because Ronna called last night. I was hoping she would call to wish me a happy birthday; I had been hurt by not getting a card from her, but the call more than made up for it. Ronna said I am a very accomplished person for a 24-year-old; coming from her, it was high praise indeed, even tho she said that years ago I looked like a very unlikely candidate for any kind of success.

Ronna's still in a terrible quandary about quitting the publishing company. Gwen is her friend, & Ronna doesn't want to leave Gwen & Cathy in the lurch; if Ronna quits, her tightwad boss Mr. Gladstone may eliminate her position, & then the workload on the other two women would be enormous.

Neither Ronna nor I mentioned last week's conversation; we were really clicking last night & when she asked if she could see me this Sunday, I quickly said, "That would be great." So perhaps Ronna & I can yet be friends & sometime lovers. I realize now that my not having a girlfriend these past 7 months has been one factor in my literary output. So I don't think I'd want a full-time girlfriend now; I'd rather concentrate on myself & my writing, selfish as that may be. (I told Ronna last night: "I am the most selfish person I know.")

There was a birthday cake from Carvel's for me last night - just the five of us, & it was pleasant. There were the little jokes & family talk, & it all seemed like

something I'll be nostalgic for one day: Dad being on
a diet, Jonny talking about his golf swing, Marc trying
to explain to a very dense older brother how color TV
works, Mom cutting the cake the way she always
does: making a circle inside the cake with a knife
dipped in water & then slicing the pieces. Twenty-
four candles are a lot; I could not blow them out with
one breath. I wished for a teaching job in the fall, &
Dad guessed my wish. I called up both sets of
grandparents to thank them for my gifts.

Alice came over this morning with what she says is
"the first half" of my birthday present: a collection of
poems by & an interview with Erica Jong (the book
inscribed: "May you be as rich & famous as Erica!").
Alice brought us ice cream, & we talked in my
bedroom for hours. Tomorrow, after her graduation
from Fordham, she's going to see the editor of the
Sunday News Magazine; he's going to help her fix up
a story she wrote having to do with the theft of her
brother's stamp collection. Alice's article on Mr.
Blumstein will be out in Flatbush Life next week; I
don't think our old Spanish teacher is going to be
entirely happy with it because he may feel
embarrassed. Andreas was supposed to take Alice
away for the weekend, but he'll be busy working on a
sculpture for some church's competition.

Tuesday, June 6, 1972

Sometimes things happen so fast I wish I had time to catch my breath. It was a cool, cloudy day - not too hot or too humid. I arrived on campus this morning to find the talk in LaG again centered on politics - 'tis the season. Elspeth came in with a red, white & blue Larry Simon umbrella. I see that man's face everywhere, on buses, posters, in newspapers. But despite the lavish expenses and the work of Jerry, Shelli, Doc, Marty, Mason, etc., I hear the campaign is floundering. Late tonight come the big results from the Calif. primary - which could give the whole show to McGov.

I talked with Mike as I walked with him to move his car & confided in him about Avis's card. He termed it "a proposition if I've ever heard one." I suppose it was sort of saying she wants me to sleep with her. I've wanted her for so long, so futilely, I find it hard to believe. And her writing about my being "too sweet," Mike said that I can't say "fuck it" to some people - & then I get hurt too easily.

In Drama, we had a great discussion on Ibsen's *A Doll's House*; at one point, Prof. Galin remarked that "you have to learn to be alone before you can be with people." Coming toward LaG, I saw Leon sitting on the steps with...Greg, who looks slimier and more dissipated than ever. Greg was telling Leon about Madison - Leon's got to decide whether to go to

Wisconsin or Chicago for grad school in Sept.

I went to lunch with Elayne & Elspeth, & coming out of Campus Corner, I saw Avis walking a stroller with the baby she's been "sitting on," as she calls it. She showed me a letter Scott wrote to both of us. He's doing fine but is a bit lonely & scared. (Tonight I wrote him.)

Avis & I took the baby to the playground, where we played on the swings & watched him pull leaves from bushes & hugged him & talked. There was a moment when the baby walked away & Avis turned to me & I looked at her directly & things got so weird & heavy I had to turn away.

I told her I'd call her & went to Dr. Wouk, where I got a mild jolt. My shrink announced that he's leaving NY City & his practice for good, in 2 weeks. Dr. Wouk thinks I should continue with therapy & will refer me to somebody else. But, wow, after 3 years, how am I going to relate to someone else? Dr. Wouk has been a constancy to me & soon he'll be gone.

Thursday, June 7, 1973

5 PM. I feel a bit like Dustin Hoffman in "The Graduate": for the past few days I've been loafing by the pool, getting a sunburn, indulging myself - but I'm not really happy doing that. I have to keep moving, get started on some new goal. Perhaps that's

the curse of being achievement-oriented; once I've completed something, I feel aimless. I have *everything*, I guess: a nice house, all the possessions I want, a not unsympathetic family, a girl who loves me, a college degree & the prospect of a comfortable future - but I'm still dissatisfied.

Ronna was saying last night how she could see how people can waste their lives on stupid jobs like the one she's got for the summer. You wake up early in the morning, go do your mind-rotting tasks all day, fight the rush hour traffic home, & by then you're too exhausted to do anything but sleep in preparation for the same thing the next day. But Ronna's job is only a temporary thing, & my...my drifting is also only a temporary summer thing.

I got a birthday card from Alice today, postmarked London. She writes that she'll be home this week after seeing Madrid. I miss her, perhaps because she's my oldest friend & provides a sense of stability & continuity that no one else can.

I went to bed early last night & was nearly comatose for 12 hours. This morning, I stopped by the college for a minute - yes, it's hard to break away - it was deserted. So I drove uptown to see a movie with my student discount pass: Bogdanovich's "Paper Moon," a lovely, old-fashioned kind of picture about the 30's. I can see how easy it is for people like Stanley to escape into celluloid. I crossed 3rd Ave. & looked around in Bloomingdale's, then drove to downtown Bklyn to have lunch at Junior's. It was a pleasant enough day, but I feel so restless & a bit under the weather. I've got to see Mrs. Ehrlich tonight.

Monday, June 8, 1970

A sunshiny day. Mom gave me the car this morning & I drove downtown. Dr. Wouk & I got into heavy stuff after he showed me some of the tricks his dog Psyche does. I've been trying to hide my sexual feelings, be asexual & ethereal & it just can't work. Which way will I turn - to the gay life or to the straight world? Dr. Wouk says there's no hurry but that I don't want to jerk off my whole life, that I need love. What can I do? Gay bars, dating girls, the beach, computer dating? I'm gay, so would it be fair to see girls? Altho I've never acted out any fantasies, I know, or rather, I feel at least 70% homosexual. Maybe I should contact Brad or Carlos again - but answering their ads, tho, were probably once-in-a-lifetime things. Sometimes I wonder if I've gotten anything at all out of therapy.

At home, I took little Scotty to Georgetowne, where I bought lemon hair lightener. It worked a bit as I sat in the back, reading Thomas Mann & Erik Erikson. Mom & Dad were quarreling at dinner, Marc was grouchy & Jonny was bitchy. Marty called Monticello & learned Space Age came in 2nd on Saturday. Mom went over to the Cohens' & Dad went to 86th St.

because Pat became sick & the new manager, Marc, was left alone in the store until Dad came.

Tomorrow I start my job. I'm sure I can handle it. It's what Dr. Wouk called an "assistant Puerto Rican" position. I've got to start writing again - facing myself is good if difficult. I've been living the life of a boy & not the life of a man.

Sunday, June 9, 1974

11 PM. Things have settled down somewhat, but I still am finding life enormously interesting. I just watched a program by Barbara Walters on the sexual problems of men. (Freudian-slippingly, I nearly stopped the pen after the "e" in "men". Of course I have a lot of sexual hangups but as things become freer - both in society & within myself - things will get better.) At least that whole "macho" mystique is dying away, except in the mind of self-styled studs like Costas.

Last night I was very satisfied, & if Ronna didn't have an orgasm, it happens often enough to satisfy her, she said; it's not like being on a playing field. It's a relief to have many people realize that a guy isn't always ready to have sex any more than a woman is. Today I could handle my impotence with Stacy with honesty & openness & I wouldn't have to go thru the trauma & embarrassment I felt back in October '72.

Ronna starts summer school tomorrow, taking Soc &

English courses relating to American Studies. After seeing Ronna on TV, Mom told me, "You don't know what you've got" - but I *do* realize what a great person Ms. Ronna is. Speaking of openness, remember Harold, Ronna's mother's erstwhile fiancé? It turns out that he had made up not only his son's accident & his flight to London to see the boy, but also the son as well! He fabricated the whole story about having an ex-wife & children in England, his career as an Army major, his job, his entire life. What a sickie! He called up Ronna's mother recently & said now he could be honest, but she quickly hung up on him. Ronna, it seems, was right all along in her suspicions about the man, & her mother now admits that. So do I.

Alice came over this afternoon on her trusty bike, bringing me delicious presents (an Indian flute & a German set of tiddlywinks, purchased at the B'klyn Museum) as well as a hand-made birthday card from Mark, "to the best reporter I ever had, from the best editor you ever had." He told me to call him, & I was trying his phone all evening but got no response.

Alice told me some horror stories about her school, like the one about the 6'4" 8th grader named Mario who's stabbed 8 people already, & John, who steals street cleaning vehicles & calls Alice "Gorgeous." Alice said she spent a masochist day yesterday. In the afternoon she biked with Hal, who said he feels like Marlowe in *Heart of Darkness* & who finds his brother Bob "morally perfect." And then she spent last evening with Renee, who's depressed because she doesn't have an escort to her sister's wedding to a guy named Tevye Ratz.

We talked for hours about little things which seemed fascinating at the time. Alice went to a show with Peter on Thursday & he said that Wednesday's party depressed him, I guess because he felt out-of-place with all the new people. I told Alice thank you for the gifts & said I'd see her this summer; she'll be going to Richmond, mostly.

It was very hot today & the pool was finally set up, so I went in with the family & Fern. Fern is a very sweet girl; last night she & Marc went with her parents to see "Damn Yankees." Gary had told me he & Kathy enjoyed it very much, too. Gary left yesterday for Guard training at Fort Drum; he'll be back in 2 weeks & hopes to see more of that girl.

I've been doing a lot of thinking about "The Peacock Room," making up dialogue, thinking out symbols, playing with my characters. I hope to finish the story by September & school. Avis said her friend Julie's sister Barbra will also be in the BC MFA program. She's 24 & spent a year in her house, as I did.

Thursday, June 10, 1971

A mild, bright day. Getting up so early in the morning isn't easy & I haven't been able to get used to it as of yet. Shelli called me late last night, very upset. I was half-asleep & told her stupid things so this morning I called her to make sure she was all right - she was. We met in school before classes - we sat in LaGuardia lobby with Richie. In Poli Sci, we started to go into party organizations, & it's more interesting altho I was so tired, I had a hard time keeping awake. After class, I shared a peanut butter & jelly sandwich with Leon. Elspeth wants to come with me to see Elihu off on Sunday - she didn't mention the fact that Jerry was also leaving then.

I wanted to stay and talk with Juan & Mike, but Shelli wanted to go home. At home, she made us salads, then we went upstairs to my bedroom to make love. It was fantastic today, very earthy & real. It was a bit too cool to do any swimming, so we went to Georgetowne, where we had coffee. Shelli has been on a strict diet all week & it's making her not herself. But she's been hurt a lot because of her weight & if she can lick the problem, it'll be worth it.

Shelli got me a gift subscription to New York Magazine. I was reading about the revival (by Bella Abzug) of the Mailer-Breslin scheme for making NYC the 51st state. A drive is on for secession & with the recent developments, it's gotten a lot of publicity.

We went to the Marine & saw a double feature: "Little Murders," a wild movie about violence & feelings in the city, based on the Feiffer play, & "Making It," about a high school kid's sexual adventures. Shelli was upset by the abortion scene in the last movie - she may take the pill after all.

I called Brad. He's now working at St. Vincent's Hospital & was rejected from medical school. We rapped for half an hour about impersonal things. He said to keep in touch by phone but he never expects to see me in person again.

Wednesday, June 11, 1975

I needn't have worried about becoming smug & overconfident. By tonight I'm practically brimming over with self-doubt. Two rejection notices didn't help: one from the Long Island Review, a form letter, & from The Smith, a neatly typed note that says, "Thank you & good luck." But I guess I needed a little humility, right? I was going to be the Man to Save the Novel. Let's just see if I can save my own life. I am becoming a little bored, & I would like to be working. It would be better for my self-esteem even tho I have money in the bank & have been as stingy with myself as a constipated spinster.

Speaking of that, I called Vito today & we had a nice chat. He said it's now a year since his stay in the hospital & he ventured that if he ever got the idea to commit suicide, he'd do it by constipating himself to death. He'll be going to summer school at BC when the graduate session begins. Right now he's movie-hopping, at least until the end of the week when the Rugoff passes run out. Vito asked me if I wanted to go to the premiere of "Nashville" with him today, but I spent my discount last night when I saw "Monty Python & the Holy Grail" at Cinema 1 - it was fairly amusing.

But I was in a bad mood after weathering miserable Manhattan traffic & an acid stomach compounded by my inability to get into the new Woody Allen film. I strode down 3rd Avenue, fuming. A passing woman gave me a chance to ventilate my wrath when she asked if she could "borrow some change." "What do I look like, Rockefeller?" I shouted at her madly. "Go get a job, you good-for-nothing bum! It's people like you who are ruining the city!" Etc. etc. until she slunk away. Passing people were probably convinced I was viciously maligning some unfortunate old soul, but I didn't give a shit.

Anyhow, getting back to Vito, he was in fine fettle; he thought my story about Scott & Elspeth was "a classic"; he said that Helen's been seeing a lot of Mason but that she may see Frank after all (apparently there was a falling-out between them). Vito's family is all fine, he said; his brother stayed out on a date last night till 3 AM & Vito was waiting up for him like an anxious father. Mario & Tony are OK, too. God knows where Vito gets the money to see every show & film in town, even the ones that are all impossible to get tickets for. It was good to hear from Vito again, & I must see him soon.

After hanging up with him, I dialed Mavis's phone number; she was just on her way out, to meet Helen & Grace at Brighton Beach. I told her to stay up & I'd be right over to pick her up. Mavis went to Washington over the weekend to visit Phyllis, who's working there over the summer, & she saw the Univ. of Maryland & was favorably impressed, as that about makes her mind up about grad school. She said graduation was one big bore, & as we drove she took photos of me with Bob's camera.

We finally found a parking space & then met Helen & Grace on the beach; they were sitting with Grace's grandmother, who only speaks Spanish. It was great to see Helen again; she's gotten thinner & I noticed she bleached the hairs on her chin. Helen also seems very mellow, as befits a Californian; she was very interested in my MFA program. From her conversation, I gathered she was seeing a great deal of Mason -- she & Grace were planning to go to his house this weekend. I know that Mason's always been terribly fond of her, & that's understandable. Grace was her usual sprightly & quirky self; she's going to summer school at BC. Her abuela is funny too. We sat out on the beach for an hour or so, then Mavis & I left, as she had to meet Bob in the city at 4:30. Mavis will be going to that camp in Honesdale, Pa., in 2 weeks, so we made tentative plans to see each other before her departure. It would be nice to see Helen again before she leaves for the West Coast, but I'm glad I didn't miss her altogether. Quite a few of my friendships & acquaintanceships need patching up, & it's good to work on that.

Friday, June 12, 1970

A very humid, cloudy day. I didn't feel well this morning so I didn't go to Eikenberry HQ as planned. Instead, I stayed home & finished Newfield's book, a beautiful portrait of a great man. Robert Kennedy was an existential hero & could have helped us so much.

This afternoon I drove out to the college, but few people were around. Mark took me up to the office & for an hour he taught me about journalism: lead stories, headlines, doing interviews. Mark & I get along famously & sometimes I think he sees me as a protege. I picked up Jonny at school, then went over & chatted with the Cohens for a bit. At home again, I finally wrote my long-delayed letter to Barbara; I hope she forgives me for not writing sooner.

I thought of trying out for the play Leroy was talking about but decided against it. Acting makes me very nervous, altho I like the sense of community among theater folk. Miss Wachsberger gave me a P in Art -

her card arrived today.

Driving around tonight, I saw Marv walking with a friend, & he returned my wave. Last night I got out last year's diary & added to the quotes I've been saving - I love to look at them. I've been feeling hopeful lately.

Margaret Mead was on TV tonight & she was fascinating. Fighting continues in Jordan between the gov't & the commandos. Tonight I started reading Martin Luther King's *Where Do We Go From Here?*

Tuesday, June 13, 1972

I got the car back tonight, & after dinner I test-drove it out to Rockaway. I parked it on the first street you can park legally on in Neponsit & walked to the beach. I guess I'm sort of taking a leaf out of Mikey's book, as he often takes long walks along the beach. It's a good place to think, especially when the sun is setting: it's really beautiful & I was alone except for two boys frolicking in the water. I walked past Ivan's block, kind of hoping to see him - & yet if I had, would I have gone over to talk with him? I think not.

Avis said Shelli told her, referring to me, "How can you just have no contact with someone you were so close to?" Avis answered, quite rightly, "That's the way life goes." The water seems to make things clear & I thought about what Dr. Wouk & I talked about in our next-to-last session this afternoon. He thinks a lot of what Elspeth & Avis said about Shelli thinking about me is bullshit, that they may be jealous of Shelli being married. Perhaps I wanted it to be so - it's ego-gratifying to think that your married ex-girlfriend can't forget you. She's probably much too busy to give me more than a passing thought, & that's the way it should be. Dr. Wouk said it's high time I had another girlfriend, & I agree, but it's not easy to find the right person. He asked one thing of me, that I invite him to my wedding.

My trip to Miami for the Convention is uppermost in my mind right now. I'm apprehensive about it, but it's something I really want to do, to be a part of history & politics & *life* - the best play of the year, so to speak. This morning I saw Mark at school. *Brooklyn Today* came out today with an article by him. I had him put me down for a subscription. He's really a fine, gentle person even if I don't agree with his lifestyle. Mark was so proud when he told me that Conseulo was 3 mos. pregnant; I didn't have the heart to tell him I knew already & pretended to be surprised. English went rather well today, & I came home early - I got a ride home with Charles, who said Leon's film turned out very well, so far as he can see. And I declined an invitation to join a camping trip to Split Rock with Leon, Skip, Elspeth, Jessie, Allan & Josh – a weird assortment of people even if they are all my friends.

Wednesday, June 14, 1972

I feel quite depressed tonight & there's no reason for it. I've been fighting off waves of nausea, so perhaps it's something physical, say a stomach virus. But more likely it's just a passing, momentary thing. I awoke this morning from a night of heavy dreams to a dark, cool day. I took the car to school & arrived on campus at 10 AM. Mike, Mikey & I went to Campus Corner (they had lunch, I had rose hips tea) & we bullshitted as always. It's strange how you become close with people, but it's a good feeling: to know that there are people you can talk with about anything. We joke & kid & help each other. Slade once wrote in his Kingsman column that "friends slow down hell," & they certainly do do that, at least for me.

We had another good discussion in class, this time on Synge's "Riders to the Sea," a play I found primeval & comforting. After class, Prof. Galin told me I've been really helping him out with my comments. I felt very flattered.

I found Leon in front of LaG & gave him his birthday present: the children's book Alice got me (not the same copy, of course) & an autographed photo of William Scranton. I sat with Ken & Skip & John & enjoyed their chatter. I think Leon's getting into the gay bag, as Skip keeps prostelytizing for homosexuality. But Leon told Skip not to bring along acid on the camping trip; Leon's not tripping any more after a bad experience.

I went to lunch with Elayne, a congenial meal partner, & then met Allan. Allan doesn't like his typing job & is looking for another one - at least he's not mad at me anymore. Back home, I found a card from London, from Alice. London, she writes, will never make her "top 10 list: weather gloppy, uninteresting food & a 6th floor walkup shared with 2 80-yr-olds & an Irish girl who doesn't speak much & looks at me funny - so far she's kept her distance." I spoke with Gary for a while, then Avis called & she seduced me into cutting school tom'w & doing something with her. I went down to McGovern HQ & worked, writing down phone numbers of people already canvassed who favored McGovern, so we can call them up on Primary Day.

Saturday, June 15, 1974

It's difficult to take responsibility for your feelings, but more often than not it's satisfying in the long run. I remember in group therapy with Dr. Lippmann, a girl became annoyed with me because "All we know about you is that your mother hates when you walk on the living room carpet & so you do it to annoy her!" I did hide behind intellectualizing in those days, but what I told the group was still important. I'd been brought up to believe that what looked nice and "proper" was more important than feelings & instincts, & my walking on the carpet was more than adolescent spite: I was telling my parents that I would not submit to not feeling. Even my anxiety attacks were a kind of rebellion, as my body *forced* me to listen to it.

Things started rough with Ronna last evening. We knew we had to talk, so I drove unconsciously & told Ronna that I wanted to sleep with other people, males & females, that I don't want to marry her or even live with her, & I tried to find out how she felt about our relationship & how we stand a month after our Mother's Day talk. At times I felt I was reaching out to her & she wasn't there - she had her head turned, looking out the window. I guess it's harder for her to trust me than vice versa. But after a long, difficult talk, she finally told me that she felt much the same way as I did altho she admitted to being a bit hurt because I don't love her passionately. (She said, tho, that this is probably more comfortable.) She didn't seem shocked or disgusted by homosexual inclinations & said it doesn't make me any less of a man in her eyes, maybe more of a man because I'm honest with myself. We talked a long time & took deep breaths & after awhile, we both felt better.

Ronna & I decided to go to B'klyn Heights - it was still daylight at 8 PM. I parked on Remsen St., by Shelley Wouk's old office, now adorned with a sign that says "Somebody, M.S.W., Primal Therapy." We took in the shops around Montague St. There was a beautiful sign in a florist's window, a sort of essay called

"Diversity, Thy Name is Life," talking about how wonderful the differences between people are & how they should not lead to hate but love. There were those trendy stores & tea shoppes & cheese places & the sidewalk cafes. Children were playing & people were walking their dogs.

We strolled the length of the Promenade, holding hands & staring at the river & the Manhattan skyline. We walked along Willow St., looking for Norman Mailer, & Ronna pointed out Mona's old apartment on Pierrepont: she & Ivan broke up there one night when they baby-sat for his niece. We got root beer ice cream at Baskin-Robbins, & it started to get dark so we went back to Canarsie, where I gave her my parents' graduation gift: a music box for jewelry. Her mother gave me a *Writer's Market '74*, something I could really use; maybe I'll even sell some stories.

We were alone in her room & made love. She let me do some things for the first time. We lay on the couch a long time & I felt good & calm & clean. I left at 2 AM, came home & fell asleep right away.

Josh called today to ask me if I wanted to buy Earth Shoes with him, but I declined without feeling guilty about it (another step forward!). I got my new TV set today, & I called Joey to wish him a happy sixth birthday. My godson is growing up; hopefully, he'll be happy.

Wednesday, June 16, 1971

It was cool & cloudy this morning, but it turned fair & sunny later in the afternoon. I met Avis early this morning. Stacy called her up last night & asked her if she wanted to go to Scandinavia. So, after the term ends, Avis & Stacy will go to Europe. Alice said she's leaving for Spain in two weeks. Unfortunately, it's the day of Shelli's sister's wedding, so we can't see her off at the airport. Shelli came by & said the preparations for the wedding are getting more hectic day by day.

In Poli Sci, we again had an interesting discussion. The gov't got an injunction against the Times & they can't print any more of the Pentagon Vietnam report. I joined the summer crowd on the steps of LaGuardia after class. Slade is very interested in becoming the editor of the Spigot, & I think it would be great. And so does Elspeth, who has a huge crush on Slade, who is pretty sexy, I must admit.

Gary still doesn't know how his mother found out about the party. Shelli & I were going to lunch, & I asked Gary to join us, hoping he'd refuse. But he came along & spent a half-hour boring us with that faulty diction, those malapropisms of his. He conferred with Allan & has decided to have the party on the beach in Neponsit. There are so many problems with that, but I'm glad that he stopped trying to talk me into having the party at my house.

Shelli & I went home to bed, & I don't know why, but it wasn't terrific today. I was edgy for some reason & she was tense, as she had to see Dr. Russell. But it was still wonderful. I did my Poli Sci paper & I think it's pretty good, but I'm wary of Prof. Gluck. I took Shelli to the college, we had coffee & I dropped her at her shrink's. Then I went home, did some work & picked her up at SUBO. We drove to Prospect Park & walked & watched the sun set. I think Mom found my condom boxes, but she didn't say anything. But I feel strange, like that time she called Dr. Wouk asking if I was gay.

Tonight I made a birthday card for Leon, using quotes from my 1969 diary. I realize now that I like Leon, & maybe, just maybe, I could have loved him.

Sunday, June 17, 1973

It's Sunday evening, the beginning & end of a week, a good time for taking stock. It's two weeks since my graduation & I've managed to survive, maybe even thrive. I've had diarrhea for the past three days, but I'm sure that it's only a psychological reflection of my emotional uncertainty. This leisurely gadding about has been fine, but it can't go on much longer: I've got to make some kind of future for myself.

So I've made some tentative decisions. First, I'm going to register at Richmond for the summer on Thursday & go there in the fall unless I discover it's really horrid. I started looking at the apartment ads, but I don't want to move out until the end of summer. And I've decided that I'm very much in love with Ronna. I found a long reddish-brown strand of hair on my bed, & I remember the smell of her body, her firm plumpness (I suppose I have old-fashioned tastes in women), & even more, her gentle humor, honesty & earnestness. She says she's happy to continue just as we are, with no thought to the future, & so am I. Well, that's good enough for one day's thought-work.

A cool Father's Day. I gave Dad his present - he liked it a lot - & then went to Rockaway to see Grandpa Herb (I couldn't get to see Grandpa Nat because he wasn't home). Today was Mikey's barbecue. Ronna couldn't make it because she was with her father, so I went alone, stopping off on the way from my grandparents' to Carvel's to get an ice-cream cake that said "Happy Anniversary Watergate" since a year ago the break-in occurred. Everyone appreciated it.

Bill was there but left early - he stayed a week with Allan in Tampa & is working at a construction site. Most of the people there were friends of Mikey & Mike who live in Rockaway or go to Buffalo: Helene; Charles; Rhonda, a vacuous redhead; a few others including Neal from Calling Card. Mike showed me a letter from Pres. Kneller (obviously written by Holly) which refused to "certify" him because of the 30% BHE rule but "appointing" him & Linda as Kneller's "designees" to take over SG. I spoke with Felicia, who seems sweet if a little dull. But perhaps that's unfair; I don't know her. The food was great, & I enjoyed the company, & Mikey's mom was her usual gracious self.

Friday, June 18, 1971

It was cool & cloudy this morning as I went downtown to see Dr. Wouk. Before I went in, I walked around by the Manhattan Bridge. The sky was darkening & everything was filled with a kind of luminescence. Dr. Wouk said he's a follower of Ayn Rand & I should be selfish. He said it was very important not to change. I must not give in to Shelli on this or she'll change me to be her pet cipher. He said I should be proud to be a male chauvinist as he is. To tell you the truth, I think he's full of shit, but I listened politely & said I'd see him next week, before he went away.

It was raining when I got out & I went into the Slack Bar to visit Grandpa Herb. He & Grandma are leaving next Monday for Canada. I had lunch at home & then Avis came over, early, as usual. She & Stacy set back their departure until next Friday because Stacy broke her toe. Avis said that Scott separated from Roger & Lewis & went to L.A. by himself.

Shelli came soon after, bringing a card that said "thank you for being you." When I told her about Dr. Wouk, she dialed his number & shouted "Pig!" into the phone. She was upset, & as the three of us went to Kings Plaza & looked around, both she & Avis tried to convince me that Dr. Wouk is a nut. I'm very confused at the moment.

We went to the movies to see "Summer of '42," a pretty good film about a teenage boy's growing up during World War II. Avis took the bus home, & Shelli & I came back to my house. We lay in bed, not having sex, but just hugging & kissing in each other's arms. I do love her very much - very much. She told me that on the phone Saul had said he still loved her & wanted to see her alone, not with me. Despite all the things that are pulling us apart or trying to, anyway, I know Shelli & I are right for one another. I reluctantly took her home, giving her a long passionate goodbye kiss.

I called Carole, who still isn't feeling well. She said that she went to Homowack with Hymie for the weekend. There she met Elayne, who told her Mark & Consuelo are having a baby. Avi asked me to come to a meeting of "key" Spigot staff members tomorrow. What's he got up his sleeve?

Friday, June 19, 1970

A rough, humid day. I went to Eikenberry HQ in the Heights this morning & licked stamps for a mailing that's going out tonight. On the IRT going back to school, I ran into Juan, back from his parents' in

Panama, & we went to the office together. Mark was at his desk & showed me how to copyedit. He left to see an orthopedist - he's trying to use his trick knee to get out of the draft. It was sunny for a bit, & I went into the backyard & began reading Galsworthy's *Maid in Waiting*.

There was a rally at the Junction at 5:30. I saw Adam Walinsky there, but he didn't quite know me. Adam seems very nervous about his chances. After I said I'd been talking him up, he asked me, "But do they know who I am?" I still respect him greatly & he made a fine speech. Basil Paterson spoke against Con Ed & Ma Bell, & seemed popular with the crowd. By mistake, Adam was introduced as "the next Att'y Gen. of the U.S." - I wish he was. It started to rain heavily & they said Goldberg was delayed indefinitely so I left.

Dad went to the track with Sid tonight. Grandpa Herb called & Mom & I went to him at the toll bridge. He skidded in the heavy rain, ran into a fence & got 2 flat tires. We drove him to the gas station - he was soaked & shaken but unhurt - where they fixed the tires. Mom drove him back to the bridge & Grandpa got home safely. He's lucky he wasn't killed.

It looks like a real upset tonight in Britain as the Conservatives may have toppled Harold Wilson's Labour government.

Friday, June 20, 1975

9 PM. I was just noticing how light it is at this hour, & then I realized that we're approaching the summer solstice. After Sunday, it will officially be summer & the days will begin to get shorter. I was working on "A Sophomore's Diary: April 1971" last night & today. I had to make a list fictionalizing the 75 or so names that appear in the diary - I don't want to slip & inadvertently put down a real person's name. For it is fiction - a tenuous kind of fiction, to be sure, but I'm withholding my judgment until I've completed transposing the diary into a fictional manuscript.

Actually, I'm certain it's my reading of Manuel Puig & my admiration for his narrative techniques which made me try this experiment. I don't really expect anyone to follow 90% of the "characters" - on the first 3 pages of the story, I introduce about 30 names, & that's all most of them are, just names. But it does give me a feeling of movement, of the kind of circus that LaGuardia Hall was. And doing this is a kind of self-analysis for me. I look back & see an intensely romantic young sophomore, caught up in a clinging neurotic relationship; a person terribly concerned with listing people's names as a kind of show of his own worth (the more friends you have, the better you are); a phobic guy, totally out of touch with his feelings, panicked by his own homosexual desires, unsure about enjoying his first sexual adventures with a girl; a boy who wants recognition & who is essentially a manipulator. In these 4 years I've changed & I haven't changed. At least I hope my writing style has become more sophisticated; the 19-year-old me would be hurt to know that I find his earnestness & emotional outpourings rather funny. Yet it's affectionate, gentle laughter, & perhaps the 1971 Richie would understand.

I overslept & missed Jonny's graduation from junior high this morning; it was at 9 AM & I just couldn't rouse myself. Dad took the day off & later took Jonny to play golf, which is my littlest brother's sole passion these days. Marc's been home with a vague illness past couple of days; he says he feels very weak. I bicycled over to Harry's this afternoon, & he invited me up to his porch. He was sitting, wearing only shorts, of course, with a woman I recognized vaguely. Even with my bad eyesight I know she wasn't Fran, & it turned out she was Annie, Marv's little sister: we met several years ago at a party given by Julie, Harry's then-girlfriend. Evidently Annie's still friendly with Julie, & what Harry's relationship with her is, I can only guess, & I really am trying to give up gossip. There's nothing wrong with Harry & Fran having an open marriage. Fran always struck me as a very wise woman & she has learned by now how to live as Mrs. Harry.

He was disappointed when I told him Ronna & I are no longer seeing each other. "She's probably the only girl who was in my car for 12 hours & still came out a virgin," Harry said. Harry & Annie are planning on taking a camping trip to the Adirondacks & asked if I'd be interested in joining them, just the three of us. I told them I wasn't much for camping out but maybe Ronna might want to come along with them, as I know how much she enjoyed her many camping trips with Ivan.

Harry brought us out plates of chocolate chip ice cream as I stroked the head of his friendly little dog. I get along great with the dogs of all of Ronna's old boyfriends - as I did yesterday with Tiger. Harry has begun writing stories again; the first one he wrote this summer is about a married man who screws around. I wonder where he got *that* idea from. Actually, I think most of Harry's fiction is autobiographical, first-person narrative. When he was an undergraduate, Baumbach dug only his violent scenes, Harry said. That sounds exactly like both Jon & Harry. He mentioned getting a mouthpiece yesterday, so I assume he's still boxing; one of these days I should ask him to teach me something. Annie & Harry were very pleasant companions to while away a spring/summer afternoon with, & I'd like to see more of them.

Thursday, June 21, 1973

It's late afternoon on the first day of summer & there's a thunderstorm outside; it's hot & muggy. Today was the day I registered for the summer

session at Richmond College & my first real feeling of
what it's going to be like there as an M.A. student.
First of all, I feel proud to report that the strange new
experience didn't leave me a mass of anxious
bewilderment. I think I let my instincts & curiosity
take over.

I timed the drive at 45 minutes, so I figure I'll give
myself an hour for traveling each way. The drive is
pleasant, along the Belt P'kwy onto the Verrazano
Bridge & up Bay St. along the waterfront to St.
George. The ferry is a block away, & faded mansions
line the side streets. Boro Hall & the courthouse are
across the street from the main building, a 9-story, air-
conditioned modern office-type building.

The school is an upper division college, starting at the
junior year, & seems to be one of CUNY's more
experimental schools. There are no departments, just
divisions, no letter grades but Pass, Honors & Fail, &
the curriculum is rather experimental & disorganized.
I went to the Humanities Division to talk briefly with
the adviser, Prof. Cullen. When I asked the secretary
if I needed an appointment, she laughed & said, "No
one needs an appointment to see Pat Cullen." Indeed,
I found him to be informal; he looked like Mark,
younger than me even. I'm going to have him for a
teacher for Victorian Poetry.

I picked up the course card in the Humanities office,
then went to the cafeteria, standing on a line to give in

my personal card with the course card, until they brought my bill back from the computer. Then I paid the tuition & it was all over - relatively painless.

The President of the college has just resigned; from what I can gather, the Board of Higher Ed & most of his administration felt he was *too* liberal & too indecisive. Perhaps a change to a stricter, more traditional type of governance (like BC's Kneller) is in the offing; the students are afraid of that. But the place seems remarkably free & friendly. Faculty, administrators & students squeeze into the elevators laughing all the time, & a rubber chicken hung over the Registrar's desk.

Thursday, June 22, 1974

7 PM. I just awoke from a short nap after feeling deliciously serene & fuzzy. I awoke with an erection & the feeling I was floating. Perhaps it's because I was on the raft in the pool today. It's summer officially & in reality, *de facto* as well as *de jure*, as the lawyers say.

I had a much better time last evening than I expected to. I picked up Ronna at her house & she looked terrific, wearing this sleeveless blouse that covered up her chubbiness. We went over to her cousin's house for Barbara's 18th birthday party. I was not looking forward to spending time with such young kids & Ronna agreed that we only had to put in a token appearance, but I surprised myself by wanting to stay

the whole evening. Maybe it's because I was relaxed
& was myself, but I didn't feel a bit uncomfortable.

Ronna's Uncle Jake left for a poker game & her aunt
Violet was a visible presence, preparing watered-
down Sangria punch & cheese & chocolate fondue.
Ronna had been over there earlier in the day to bake
some sour cream bread, which was very delicious.
Ronna is talented in the kitchen. Her little cousin Al
was around, getting underfoot & instigating
everywhere. Ronna asked Barbara how she was
feeling & Barbara replied that she still got tired a lot &
often had sick headaches. Even Barbara has come to
believe that her illness is psychogenic in origin; she
doesn't get on at all well with her grandmother
Minnie, with whom she shares a room.

I had met some of Barbara's girlfriends in the hospital
& I remembered her friend Tom from seeing him in
"Arsenic & Old Lace" & meeting him when we saw
"Women in Love" at BC. "That was good," Tom said,
& I replied, "Seeing the movie or meeting me?" & after
that, we got along really well. My guess is he's
definitely gay or at least bisexual. He's an opera freak,
so I immediately thought of fixing him up with Tony
(God, am I a busybody), likes "All About Eve"
(somehow I knew he would when Ronna & I were
sitting on the stairs drinking, & it reminded us of that
movie) & well-versed in politics (he says he's a cousin
of Mario Procaccino & whenever he's depressed, he
calls up Mario, who does his crying for him). It was

his overall sense of humor that made me recall my first encounter with Vito (whom I haven't heard from in a month).

As I sampled Barbara's angel food cake, I listened to her friends talking about what it would have been like in the old activist days when colleges went on strike & students took over the president's offices. I felt very old because I was *there*.

Ronna & I left at 10:30 to go back to her house. Barbara kissed me as we left - I had told her not to worry about "another year without a boyfriend" & it was an enjoyable role, like being her older brother. Susan said to me, "I'll see you later," & Tom, who was sitting on her lap, said, "Where?" Susan replied, "They're going to my sister's bedroom." I feigned embarrassment & we left.

Ronna & I went straight to her bedroom, without the usual preliminaries & got right into bed. It was heaven, really. She just looked so gorgeous, I was hungry for her touch. Ronna is letting down her guard a lot too. She seemed to have a terrific orgasm & mine must have equaled hers; it was so intense, I couldn't help moaning with pleasure. We hugged & nearly fell asleep holding each other. Later we talked - - little anecdotes & gossip. She said I smelled like I used to when we first started going out; her smell was incredibly arousing. I left at 2AM, running into Susan at the front door after Barbara's friends had dropped her off.

I spent today outside by the pool with my brothers.

Wednesday, June 23, 1971

A hazy, humid day. I still can't adjust to getting up so early - I'm afraid by the time I get used to it, I will no longer have to get up early. I'm a bit worried about Richie. He cut his gym class again today, getting into the same rut that made him fail & not graduate before. He's so wrapped up in his better transit committees & looking for a job for once - if - he graduates.

Shelli got a call late last night from her friend Brian, who goes to the U. of Florida & consequently she was tired this morning. In Poli Sci, Prof. Gluck discussed electoral behavior & such. After class, I met Alice. Andreas wants her to go to Spain & will even join her for a weekend. She said Howie really looks "terrible" now & it's obvious they no longer care for one another. Alice said she might join the Spigot, now that Slade is editor. Slade has severed his ties with Kingsman; in fact, Laura, who despises Slade, asked him to clean out his desk. I asked Slade & Mike to come back to the pool with Shelli & Elspeth & me, but Slade was busy and Mike has a bad cold. Gary was by LaG & I didn't want him to come over, so Shelli & I left early; Elspeth was to meet Jessie after her class & come to my house.

Shelli & I had sex in my room & it was cool, as it always is. We had a real good conversation with Marc afterward - he's finished with school now. Next week, when the others go away, Marc & I plan to have a good time, with cousin Scott staying over.

Then Elspeth came over & we went swimming - Elspeth enjoyed it, & I'm glad. She has a huge crush on Slade, is looking for an apartment with Ray & still likes Greg. Elspeth stopped taking the pill, tho, because she's not sleeping with anyone. She confided that she slept with another guy while she was engaged to Jerry. Jessie didn't come & went back to Elspeth's house instead. I drove Elspeth & Shelli to the Junction. Shelli later said her appointment with Dr. Russell went all right.

Daniel Ellsberg, the hawk-turned-dove mystery man who leaked the Pentagon papers (popping up in paper after paper as injunctions come out daily) had an interview in secret on TV tonight. There's more to come out, apparently.

Wednesday, June 24, 1970

The primary results were not all bad. Bella Abzug beat Farbstein & Rangel upset Powell. Badillo won, but Eikenberry lost narrowly. In our home district reformers Halperin & Sharoff beat old-line regulars.

I guess Goldberg is better than Rocky, but I don't think he can win.

My Speech teacher, Mr. Cohen, tried to allay our fears about speaking, but it just didn't work for me. I'd like to drop the course, but I'd have to take it eventually. For tomorrow, we're supposed to make a speech for 2 minutes on a gripe. My English teacher, Mr. Graves, gave us a book list but then wondered if the list was any good - his vacillation did not impress me.

Mark asked me to go to the beach with him, but I told him to come over to our pool instead. We had lunch at Wolfie's & spent the remainder of the afternoon in the backyard - I lent him a pair of shorts. Mark & I are very friendly, but it seems more of a kidding, jocular relationship than a friendship. Maybe that will change.

Dad looked better than ever as he went off to a conference of Pants Set managers at a Plainview motel. He's offering the managers a profit-sharing incentive plan. Marc's math teacher told Mom he couldn't raise his mark & advised Marc not to attend summer school - so he won't. I read some poems by Yeats for English & listened to Dr. Wouk on the Joe Franklin radio show. He makes a good guest.

Sunday, June 25, 1972

I think I have to face the fact that I'm going thru a rough time emotionally, the roughest time since those days of the breakup with Shelli. It's all so absurd - I thought I progressed so much emotionally, & now I seem to find myself in another psychic quandary centered on the trip to Miami. Frankly, I'm beginning to have severe anxiety about the trip. It'll be the first time my life that I'll really be on my own. I have so many doubts & fears, remnants of my neurotic past. Can I get thru it okay? Compounding this is my loss of Avis & Dr. Wouk, & the general feeling that I don't know where I'm going. These past weeks have been fulfilling emotionally, yet I feel depleted, as if I'd been fighting a fierce battle ending in a draw. I didn't sleep at all well - I kept thinking of Miami & the convention & Leon & Skip & Mikey. Every time I hear news about the convention, I feel a twinge of anxiety.

It was raining out - naturally - when I got up. After breakfast, I drove into Manhattan (I almost smashed up the car when I skidded wildly on the Brooklyn Bridge). I parked on E. 64th St. & 2nd Ave. & went into the Beekman Theater to see "Portnoy's Complaint." It was really a bad movie, conveying none of the bitter comic anguish of the novel, yet leaving in all the tawdry stupidity. I did like Karen Black as The Monkey, tho.

When I came out of the theater, the rain had stopped

& I strolled down Second Ave. & up Third, browsing at antique stores, buying some herbs, looking at galleries & sidewalk cafes & people. Manhattan is like a wonderland to me, a place to escape. I drove down Fifth, past Tiffany's & Bonwit Teller & the library & St. Patrick's & Dad's office. I get a good, secure feeling as I read the sign "Art Pants Co. - Marc Richards Creations." Washington Square was crowded because of the Gay-In, so I returned to B'klyn for a delicious burger at Junior's. I came home, finding Jonny ill in bed with a cold. I spoke to Avis & she'll see me tom'w - for the last time in a long time. God, I sometimes wonder if I'm not like Soames Forsyte: "He might wish & wish & never have it - all the beauty & loving in the world."

Monday, June 26, 1972

How am I doing? I'm not sure. Psychologically, I've been holding my own. Physically, I've caught a rather nasty cold (from Jonny - or from my neurosis?) Anyway, I feel slightly rotten today, which was, needless to say, another rainy, cloudy mess. Isn't it about time we had summer already?

I spoke to Gary last night. He'd spent the weekend at Lou's estate in Great Neck. It's funny: when I'm depressed, I always seem to turn to solid, dependable Gary, but at other times I treat him cavalierly. I got a call from Avis early today. She wasn't feeling well, she said - he neck was stiff & she had a bad reaction to the pill, so could I come up to her ap't instead of us meeting at school? Sure, I said.

Before class, Charles showed us the movie he'd made. It really came out well & I enjoyed it, altho I wince when I see myself on the screen. He'd showed it to Prof. Giuriceo & she'd given him an A- for it; Charles has finally graduated & wants to drop those math courses he's taking.

I walked to Flatbush Ave. with Max, this fat Poli Sci lecturer who's been hanging around. He introduced me to Liz Holtzman, who's a pretty gracious person - she was suffering with a bad cold too, so I gave her some rose hips tea. She called me "Richie" when she spoke to me; I said I'd see her in Miami.

Before I class I saw Stacy, who asked me for my address so she could write me while she & her sister are in Greece. What a strange lady! In class, we went thru "Death of a Salesman" & finished it, thankfully. I had lunch with Charles & Barry. Charles hasn't been around much, as Pauline's mother's been in the hospital.

When I got to Avis's, she was in pain with a really stiff neck - she was lopsided & so pathetically cute. She wouldn't let me crack her neck, but I massaged it & got pretty horny doing it. We sat, talking, & finally we went out to the Junction. She couldn't comb her hair, so I took a brush & brushed her long silky black hair. We browsed in card stores & bookstores & pet stores & she treated me to a soda. Back at her ap't, we talked in her bedroom. She leaves tom'w for the camp in Milford, Pa. I told her to have a nice summer as I kissed her goodbye. But I wish Avis were not going away.

Friday, June 27, 1975

5 PM. My head has cleared up a bit since yesterday. It was on the cool side today. Anyway, I finished "A Junior's Diary: Autumn 1971" last night & then had a hard time getting to sleep. A million things kept running through my mind. I thought of the Village Voice's review of the Fiction Collective's new books and their quote, "Not even the Fiction Collective always errs..." Baumbach, Spielberg & Company have such a holier-than-thou attitude, as if, to quote the Times reviewer, they were "the last of the beleaguered experimentalists" (I used that line in my last story).

I would rather reach more people than snobbily disdain the masses. As the Voice stated, if you're reading James Joyce, the difficulty is well worth it, but feebler talents like me would do better to appease the reader with some plot, characterization & continuity if they don't want their books to be junked instantly. Baumbach could make fun of the late Jacqueline Susann in a magazine article, but who in the end has the last laugh? Millions of people know or have read Susann but I doubt if .01% of them have ever heard of

Baumbach. His smugness, & Spielberg's, raise my hackles (to use a quaint cliché). I'd rather write a daytime serial & know how many people were hearing my words than write 100 Fiction Collective books.

Anyhow, I finally did cool down enough to get to sleep at 3AM or so & woke up late this morning. I'm kind of surprised, though I probably shouldn't be, that Ronna never returned my calls. I remember when I was going with her how she used to not return her other friends' calls so as to spend more time with me. Again, an instance of something I once liked about a person becomes exactly that quality that drives me up a wall. (File for future reference.) Ronna's not calling bothers me, but I realized something: I've been reacting productively and positively all along by writing. Now that I think about it, I did hardly any creative writing all the time I was seeing Shelli & then Ronna; the relationships were so intense that there wasn't enough psychic energy left over to write.

I got another non-acceptance today: the magazine folded for lack of funds. I went to BC to get my stories xeroxed & saw Josh & Barry selling plants in front of Hillel Gate. Elayne came upon me & walked me to the copy center, where I gave in my order. Elayne was on her lunch hour, so we sat down on the quadrangle & hung out. She's a bit worried that her jobs at BC & the Graduate Center are threatened by the budget cuts. I've told Elayne & Elihu about my LaGuardia stories

& they're both anxious to read them. I'm sure they have a very different conception of the writing than what it really is - it's mostly *my* story, after all.

Elihu is going on his whirlwind vacation next week. Elayne said Elihu did some "impolitic" things that got him into hot water with the Madison crowd, whom she thinks are all sickies anyway. She told me that novelist Stanley Hoffman came over to her ap't and propositioned her (they had met casually months ago at a party), using lines straight out of some bad novel. She's the third person I know who's told me a similar story; both Stacy & Karen had the same experience with the formerly fat novelist. Elayne says he doesn't even know how to kiss right, that he does it with his teeth. I'd like to meet Mr. Hoffman one day & size him up for myself; I don't think I'd like him very much, but he does sound amusing.

Mike joined us - his student teaching ended yesterday, but he has to attend lectures till the end of July. Mike said that Gary's sister's coming along & will be put in a cast soon & sent home. Melvin came over, & in response to a question from Mike, Melvin said he'll be graduating in January. "That's what you said last summer," Elayne said, & I said, "Ah, but he didn't say *which* January." Fitz dropped by with a dog that looked like a bear; he & Elayne are on good terms now that all their crises are behind them. It was fun to be with them just like in the old days. I got my xeroxed stories & came home for the rest of the afternoon.

Monday, June 28, 1971

A cool & cloudy letdown of a day. Shelli was very upset on the phone last night. The night before the wedding she & her sister stayed up all night, crying & reminiscing. And last night Sindy was with Kieran & she'll be with Kieran forever now. It's tough on Shelli. I tried to help as best I could, but I felt impotent. This morning Kieran & Sindy left for Seattle, where they'll live for the next few years. Shelli called me from the airport & said she was coming over. I awaited her & listened to the news: the shooting at the Italian-American Civil Rights Day rally of their leader, Joe Colombo, a "reputed Mafia boss."

Shelli cried in my arms when she got here - but, God, she looked beautiful, wearing a sexy white blouse & a navy blue dress. I comforted her in my room - she looked like an angel fallen from heaven. We made love & that relaxed us both, then we watched some television & talked. Every time she mentioned her sister's name, she began to cry. I told her it will be all right & I'm sure it will, that each day it will get better. She's worried about her schoolwork, but I said I'd help her with it. In the late afternoon, I drove her home. Her aunt & her aunt's stepdaughter were there but are leaving for Florida tonight.

Marc was disappointed that he only got a 75 average & Mom is worried about his getting into college. Mom spent the rest of the day preparing for her trip to Paradise Island; she, Dad & Jonny are leaving Thursday & will return next Tuesday. Dad, who told me yesterday in the car that he'd never go to the track again with Lennie, did just that tonight - despite the crackdown on the information Lennie's been getting from the paddock.

I spoke to Shelli later in the evening & she sounded better & was awaiting a phone call from her sister. I tried to speak to Elspeth, but she was working late at the dep't store. Daniel Ellsberg admitted he stole the Pentagon papers & gave himself up to the FBI.

Friday, June 29, 1973

It's odd, but I've been sort of lethargic all day & now suddenly I've perked up for no apparent reason. Later this afternoon, I decided that I was giving in to my own crankiness & that I should call somebody & do what makes me feel better: get into other people. So I called Mikey & altho we had only a brief chat, at least I got a sense other people being in the world. Mikey said Ari is enjoying med school in Guadalajara, Mason left for camp after attending a party at Stacy's with Jill, & Mikey himself will be leaving for Canada this weekend with Pauline & Charles, with whom he's been hanging around lately. And tonight I get to see Ronna, & unlike my usual pessimistic self, I think we're going to have fun.

Last night's session with Mrs. E went very well. I apologized for my verbal jousting & she asked why I have to. I'm defensive, probably because I get that as a way of dealing with Mom. She's always been, I've felt, more concerned with her possessions than with me. As I told this to Mrs. E, she noted that I kept defending my observations by using other people's, as if I were not to be trusted, that I had faulty judgment.

We talked about how my fear of being pushed out of the womb is being brought back by thoughts of moving out & of grad school. And we discussed how Prof. Cullen uses my weapon - intellectualizing - & how I was affected by his comments on Carlyle's impotence, wondering what he might see in *my* writing.

We went over that dream & 2 others in which Ivan appeared. In one, Mom had left Dad for Ivan & threatened me with knife, & in another Ronna told me I was an illegitimate son of Ivan's father, who had to pay Mom & Dad to adopt me (a reversal of real adoption & an example of my own feelings of inadequacy). I've always viewed Ivan's family as a very close-knit, loving group, but they did "give away" their only imperfection – Mona's brain-damaged daughter - which reminded me of Mom's cousin's death yesterday. At 33, Jean choked to death in an institution for the retarded. In both dreams, there was a wish that my parents weren't my parents, so I could act out Oedipal fantasies, with Ivan as a substitute for me. Mrs. E says I still fear castration (Mom's knife) & am really scared of women in general, including Mrs. E herself.

Sunday, June 30, 1974

10 PM. A rain is falling now, but it was hot & sunny all day. I just realized that the first six months of the year are almost over - half of 1974 is gone. I changed the calendar Ronna gave me to July, which is decorated with her watercolor of an orange sun, a blue sky & some birds. (June was a cutout of two teddy bears - from the wrapping paper I put her 1973 birthday presents in - with the legend "Grazin' in the grass.")

I finally got to see Ronna today. I went over to her house at noon. Ronna's cold was still with her, but her sister was much sicker, in bed with 103 fever. Ronna sounded a bit hoarse & she kept a generous supply of tissues with her for her runny nose. We drove out to Rockaway, but every parking space had been taken, even the driveway of the abandoned house across from Mikey's, so we returned to Brooklyn. Ronna told me that last night she dreamed she was in bed with both me & Ivan. We both wanted to sleep with her, but she refused, & while Ivan was disappointed, I was a bit more upset & threatened to kill her altho I didn't do it because of her pleas against murder; instead, I decided to scramble some eggs. We went back to my house - this is reality now, not the dream - & sat in the backyard by the pool.

Ronna & I were discussing Sociology (her midterm is tomorrow) & I made a beauty of a Freudian slip: instead of saying "cities," the word that came out of my mouth was "titties." I suppose it's understandable. I went into the pool & when we felt we had enough sun, we retired to my room to watch the Democratic party telethon. We hugged & kissed but made sure to avoid mouth-to-mouth contact to avoid spreading germs; keeping that distance was difficult because Ronna looked so soft and grabbable (a new word?). We sat, touching each other, & I told her it took me 22 months from the first time I saw her until I got the nerve to ask her out. Ronna said Shelli told her in the spring of '71 that I was talking about asking her out. I did it to make Shelli jealous, but there was a hint of desire for Ronna even then (Shelli told then me that if I asked Ronna out, Ivan would beat me up). But Ronna said she wouldn't have liked me then because "you were too scared to be yourself so you put on this front." Ronna said that even Melvin mentioned how much I've changed over the past couple of years. Ronna & I had lunch in the kitchen & I drove her home early, to study & rest her cold.

I went to visit Vito at Maimonides tonight; his friends, Maria & Ed, who are engaged, were already there.

Vito's mother told me the doctors finally realized the
problem wasn't orthopedic; they now think there's a
blockage in his colon or intestines. The doctors told
Mrs. M last night & she broke the news to Vito today.
"He took it well," she said. Apparently they've
thought the problem was gastrointestinal for a while.
The psychiatric nurse was brought in to help Vito
cope with the news once they saw how very high-
strung he is. I stood & joked with his friends - Maria
just graduated BC, is looking for a job & will be on a
TV game show on Thursday (she didn't win any
money). Vito was in pain, but he's off painkillers
because they're doing tests & X-rays tom'w.
Hopefully they'll do surgery before the holiday
weekend. I tried to reassure Vito & then drove home
his mother & uncle, who were very grateful for the
ride. Mrs. M is so tired. She's had a rough life & a lot
of problems, but she seems not to give in to things.

Wednesday, July 1, 1970

The second half of the year already - a warm, lazy
day. I slept soundly & was awakened by Mom from a
dream in which I was eating spaghetti & talking to
Sen. Wayne Morse. I was at school early & talked
with JC, a Polish refugee who worked with me on the
report yesterday. In Speech, Mr. Cohen showed us
how to outline our "speech to inform" - I'll spend
tomorrow preparing for my tea speech. In English, we
reviewed more of Yeats - I'm still bored altho Gil, who
had Mr. Graves, liked him immensely. I joined Mark

in the air-conditioned radicals' office & watched him mimeo something for Juan, then had lunch & browsed in the bookstore.

I came home & drove to the beach, where I lay for an hour reading magazines. I stopped off at Grandma Ethel's for a soda - she was having a card game. Going home, I decided I'd pick up a hitchhiker but couldn't find one interesting enough.

Gary writes that after bivouac, he came down with a fever. There are some complications with college & I must call his parents.

Sometimes I despair that I'll ever write anything but this diary. I'm still searching for a form & a style. Do people read fiction anymore? Will novels go the way of poetry?

My birthday was #42 in the draft lottery - I have no luck. Nixon was interviewed on network TV tonight. He named an ambassador to the Paris peace talks. Lindsay asked Howard Samuels to head the off-track betting agency.

Sunday, July 2, 1972

I woke early this morning in my hotel room in bed after a surprisingly good night's sleep. I always find it difficult to sleep in strange beds, but perhaps I'm becoming more...malleable. Actually, the whole purpose of going to South Fallsburg was to try & drive a fairly long distance myself so as to make the long trip down to Miami somewhat less awesome. I know that drive down to Florida will be a taxing nightmare for me, but of course I am prepared to be nervous, tired, headachy, faint & exhausted. Facing all this beforehand is good, I think, altho I wish I could feel differently.

I went downstairs with Jonny at 8:30 AM - like our parents, he totally loves owning a hotel - & we took a walk. The countryside was beautiful, with the dew still on the leaves & the promise of a warm day. We had a huge country breakfast in the dining room - cereal, bagels, onion rolls, grapefruit, pancakes - & afterwards I decided I'd better get going if I wanted to beat the traffic & the heat. So I packed my valise, took the car into town & got gas, then went on the Quickway back toward the city. It was a pleasant trip back, if somewhat tiresome. I arrived home at 12:15 PM, making fairly good time.

A letter was waiting for me from Scott in Sweden. He's really having a god time now. He writes that Swedish girls are "fuck-machines." Also: "You stay at home too much, Richie. I'd like to see you get away from things & leave the womb. Find yourself a woman & get *away* from things. It really makes a difference." Scott's right, of course. Perhaps that was why it upset me.

I spent the afternoon in 90-degree sunshine in the backyard, enjoying myself in my "womb." Dad came home at 5:30 & we went out for dinner at the Floridian. I spoke to Gary later. The news about his father is somewhat encouraging, thank God. Marc arrived home later in the evening, driving down from the country with a friend.

I went over to Mark's house after he called. The place was a mess, as usual, with cockroaches everywhere. Consuelo was resting & looked tired & drawn, not her usual self. I suppose it's being pregnant that does it. They decided to call the baby either David or Lisa, like the movie.

Thursday, July 3, 1975

6 PM. The July 4th holiday weekend is upon us, & I've cheered up considerably since yesterday. I slept well & was up bright & early this morning; it's becoming easier to adjust as the days go on. It's pleasant to be out in the morning before the heat of the day really wears you down. I'm enjoying my French class a lot; I just wish I had the textbook. Ms. Belfer is a marvelous teacher: interesting, witty, vibrant & entirely un-self-conscious. I was quite lucky, because Prof. Flaxman, the director of the Summer Language Institute, came in today & split up our class because it was too large. The people in the class are in a lot of different fields: there's a man getting his Ph.D. in Math, a woman going for her

doctorate in Anthropology, & Dr. Allen, a black woman who's a Psychology professor at John Jay. Taking the subways isn't so bad - I did it all the time when I was a Voice messenger in January, & most of the D trains are air-conditioned. I suppose I've always been comfortable with routines, & now that everything is becoming routinized I'm very happy.

I got an envelope from the Alumni Association containing a photo Neil took of me with Skipper Jo Davidson. I don't know if that means it's going in the Alumni Bulletin or that it's not & that's why I could have the photograph. There was no note of explanation sent with the picture.

Harry called last night, asking if he could borrow my *Writer's Market*. It seems he's been writing a lot & he wants to send out some of his stuff now. I told him to drop by anytime today & he came at 4 PM with Fran, who didn't really remember me. I think he had just picked her up from work at the hospital; she said something about supporting Harry the way my parents are supporting me. It's odd to have married people to a house that's not really mine; still, my room is mine & that's where we stayed.

I showed Harry & Fran some of my writing, & as I expected, neither of them really 'got' "Rampant Burping" or similar stuff. Harry read a good portion of my "Seance" section & he recognized most of the characters as the old LaGuardia people, who he thought were very weird. He mentioned talking to Charles, who defended Leon as a great person. It seems Harry & Fran went to North Carolina last week to see Charles & Pauline. The two women have been very close since public school; Fran said Charles is going to school for biostatistics, Pauline's working & that they have a lovely apartment & are very happy. That's good - I've always liked Charles & Pauline, & I miss them.

I asked Fran about Marc's mono & she said she had it one summer when she was very depressed about breaking up with her boyfriend of 4 years - she wasn't eating or sleeping & finally her mother made her go out & do a wash & she passed out in the laundry room. Her mono didn't show up right away, but she was ill for 6 weeks. She mentioned that having mono might give one immunity to cancer; there are some studies that indicate that.

Fran & Harry said they'd have me over to dinner - they also want to invite Ronna but I told them Ronna doesn't return my calls. Harry said he phoned her last week about going on that camping trip with him & Annie, & that Ronna said she was going on trips to Virginia & up to Cape Cod. It felt odd to hear of Ronna's plans from someone else; Fran tried to make me feel better by saying, "All girls are crazy" - she's as sweet as I remembered her. They left as it started to rain.

After 5PM, I called Scott in Washington to wish him a happy birthday. He was very glad to hear from me. Despite all of Scott's obnoxiousness, I can't stay angry with him for long. And I figured he was feeling a bit lonely; he was, & it made me feel good to be able to cheer him up a bit. All my gracious gestures are ultimately very selfish. Scott mentioned writing Avis a long letter & hopes she'll write back. I said, "I'm sure she will." We talked only a few minutes. It was 95 in Washington, & Scott's going to the 6th Annual Smoke-In on the Mall tomorrow.

Tuesday, July 4, 1972

A sunny & warm Fourth of July. I've just been outside, standing with Susan & Al, watching the neighborhood kids send up flares, Roman candles & other fireworks that make bright colors & loud noise for a while, then become nothing more than a big mess. It was giving me a headache, & so I left Susan & Al & Marc & Marilyn to watch what I think is idiocy. Still, it was a pretty nice holiday. Although the trip is in only a few days, I decided this morning to keep myself occupied & my mind too busy to worry.

So early today, right after breakfast, I drove into the city - the traffic was fairly light. I parked at Third Ave. & 58th St. & first did some shopping for herbs. Then I got in line at the Sutton Theater & went in to see "The Candidate." It was superb, the best film I've ever seen about contemporary American liberal/media politics.

Robert Redford was great as the young Democratic liberal & Don Porter came over well as his conservative Republican opponent.

I drove back into Brooklyn & enjoyed a burger with smothered onions at the counter of Junior's. When I got out of the restaurant, it was still early & nice out, so I took the car into Manhattan again. What I really wanted was a nice, sexy girl with long blonde hair & a great body - I was feeling very horny. I watched girls go up & down Fifth Avenue after I'd parked in front of the Modern Art Museum. I didn't go in, as the guards were striking & I didn't want to cross a picket line.

So I went down the block to the Museum of Contemporary Crafts & saw this odd exhibit of "American objects." I walked into St. Patrick's Cathedral & looked at the statues of the saints & the candles & stained glass. It was dark & beautifully serene. I saw in a pew for some minutes just thinking about things.

On the street I bought some ices & strolled around Rockefeller Center, then came back home at 6 PM. Mom & Jonny had come home from the hotel. Jonny said I'd gotten a call while I was away & the other person didn't say a word, just breathed. Could it be Shelli, I wonder, altho I doubt it - it's wishful thinking to imagine my married ex-girlfriend calling. Not that I like her, it's just that her calling me would be a tremendous boost to my poor ego.

Thursday, July 5, 1973

This evening I had an early session with Mrs. Ehrlich. Upon entering, I remarked how I never had seen her neighborhood in daylight before except of course when I sometimes drive by on Atlantic Ave. She wanted to know if I looked at the building then, & I said of course I do, I do it with all my friends' houses. And then I began talking about my own search for a place to live. Mrs. E detected a noticeable lack of enthusiasm for moving out on my part & altho I'd noticed it before, I never realized how much it was present.

"But I don't want people to think I'm a baby," I said, & I realized how much social pressure - by peers, today's "be on your own" philosophy, Ronna's desire to have a private place for us, my parents' wanting me to leave - was affecting my plans. I really, deep down, don't feel ready to move, & the day, August 1, that I put down as a deadline for getting an ap't, coincides almost exactly with the end of summer school & Mrs. E's vacation. Perhaps I'd better wait until the fall - to see how I like Richmond, to see about therapy, & to get some more structure into my life.

This is all bringing back feelings of when I first went

to kindergarten. I can remember how, while all the other kids around me were bawling, I wouldn't cry. Yet I must have felt the same feelings as they did, the anxiety about leaving my mother's care & being thrust into the world. I always found it extremely difficult to cry & it embarrasses me to see others do it. I feel as tho it's something shameful.

I related to Mrs. E how, during my breakup with Shelli, Dad one day came into my room & said, "You're 21 - too old to cry," & I replied, "Maybe I'm just *becoming* old enough to cry!" "Good for you!" said Mrs. E. And I use trivial incidents, like impetigo or Monday's accident to take all of my sad feelings & let them burst out. I started feeling very sad in Mrs. E's office. I was feeling the same feelings I did that first day in kindergarten & I laughed nervously, trying to change the subject so that I wouldn't cry in front of her.

Therapy is really working now. I feel as tho the therapeutic tide has turned & I'm on the road to finding out about what I'm *really* feeling.

There was a severe storm at about 6:30 this morning & our telephones were dead all day, as cables were knocked down. I spoke with Elihu last night. He told me about his dull job at Nabisco, that Elspeth had left Monday for the Coast (she's apparently going to return to N.Y.) & other gossip.

Monday, July 6, 1970

A warm, sunny day. Knock on wood, my stomach's been fine today. Mom drove me to school very early & I returned books to the library. Jose in my English class told me that he met Mr. Graves & he wasn't holding class today. In Speech, both Lou & Jessie said they missed me. I gave my tea speech & think it went fairly well.

I found Mark in the radicals' office running off something for them on the mimeo machine. We went upstairs & I helped him file documents & stuff. Mark put up a welcome mat in front of the office. We went shopping in the bookstore, then had lunch in the faculty dining room, which is a lot nicer than Boylan cafeteria.

I took a cab downtown. Dr. Wouk thinks my stomach troubles are a way of getting back at my parents for not treating me as a baby. He says that I've been struggling to return to the womb. I'm going to bring Mom & Dad in next week.

I stopped in at the Slack Bar. Marty, the manager, was in Monticello Sat. night & watched Space Age break & come in last. I took the D train & on then the Mill Basin bus home I met Barbara, who was coming from the beach.

Grandma Ethel called with sad news - George, our

old barber from Church Ave., died. So it goes.
Tonight Grandpa Herb brought over some new fish
for Marc's new fishtank. I studied for tomorrow's
Speech test & watched TV. Things seem to be looking
up. More fighting in the Middle East & Cambodia.

Wednesday, July 7, 1971

A very hot & humid day. I woke up troubled from
nightmares & went to school. Shelli called in the
morning & said she was tired & not going in. I passed
Mrs. W on the way to the bus stop, & she said Kjell is
now at a base in Virginia & will be coming home
weekends. Alice said she's going to Switzerland with
Andreas for 10 days in a couple of weeks. Avis was
very depressed with Scott away for so long; she
misses him deeply. Poli Sci was a bore - interest
group leadership. I talked to Teresa after class & she
was also down because she ran into her old boyfriend
& she's lonely. Rob took some photos of all of us. I
stayed for awhile at school, talking with Richie,
Elspeth & Jessie, then went home to have lunch.

I had a terrible sinus headache, but it cleared up when
Mom gave me the car & I picked up Shelli. We went
to the Pancake House & had a bite to eat, then roamed
thru Georgetowne - she met an old friend from public
school in the bookstore. We took a nice, long, relaxing
drive - through Prospect Park, to Sheepshead Bay,
where we stopped to get ices. Shelli got a call from
Wendy, who says she's broken up with Ronnie "for

good" - for the umpteenth time. I dropped Shelli off at her psychologist's, then went to the library, where I did some reading about the coming '72 campaign. There are so many Democrats running. I had a bad sore throat & felt a cold coming on, so I went home.

Shelli called me from SUBO. When she told her shrink about what Dr. Wouk said, Dr. Russell said she should date other guys. I began to think maybe the shrinks are right, that we're just clinging to each other neurotically, & I said she should see other boys. She hung up, crying. I sorted out my feelings in a letter to Jerry & concluded that I do love her, not neurotically but healthily. She called - I picked her up at the Junction & drove her home. We kissed & cried. She gave me a card saying "I don't love you because I need you. I need you because I love you."

Monday, July 8, 1974

When I arrived home last evening, Jonny had told me that Allan had called, so I phoned him. We had a long chat. Today he was to begin his job at the Columbia School of Business & start an evening Art course at the school (the job allows him tuition for 6 credits a semester). He said that he's angry with Mike for not driving him to the airport on his visit here last March. He's generally fed up with Mike's self-important attitude. Allan left Brooklyn thinking he had a lot of friends, & I'm afraid very few of them are left. But I guess that's what happens after an absence of 2 years.

I was awakened this morning by a call from Vito. I mistakenly thought both of the 2 phone messages were from Allan. Vito asked if I could please drive him to Canarsie to the radiologist & to Dr. Robbins, the chiropractor I recommended, & I agreed. Before going to pick up Vito & his mother, I stopped off at Hirschfeld HQ & handed in my petitions & got paid $25 in cash. It felt good to get the money. And the woman in charge said they'd call me to work at the HQ itself.

I got to Vito's house in time to help him complete dressing. Leading him down 2 flights of steps was difficult, & it was also hard to get him into my car. I drove him to the radiologist, who happened to be across the street from Ronna. I left Vito with his mother at the doctor's & rang Ronna's bell. I shared some lemonade with her - Ronna had to clean up the house today. I gathered that her mother was giving her hell for being a slob, for wasting her time taking courses & not having a job. Last night they went out to an Israeli nightclub with the family for her grandparents' wedding anniversary. I was invited too, but declined - I'm not a part of the family, after all, & I don't want to give anyone the impression that I want to be.

I hurried back to the corner. Tho the x-rays had been taken, they have to take them again on Thursday because the barium enema & so much shit is inside

Vito. They did show the spasm. We had about an hour's wait at the chiropractor. It's pathetic to see Vito struggle to walk with his cane. People on the street stare at him, & I feel so sad seeing a once-lively person so down.

Dr. Robbins is a genial, always-joking man; at first he thought I was Vito's brother. Mrs. M didn't believe in chiropractors, but I think Dr. Robbins convinced her. My parents have a lot of faith in him, & he seems to know his stuff. Vito told him the whole story, & Dr. Robbins got angry at the indifference of the doctors, saying the traction only made him worse, the Percodan could've become addictive. He was also amazed that they didn't give Vito a back injection. He gave Vito various treatments: electrodes, freezing his back with ethyl chloride, & massaging him. We were in there for over 30 minutes & the doctor gave him tips on how to go to the bathroom & how to sit. Vito is to call him tom'w to see what's what.

But Vito is still very discouraged & without hope. Perhaps it was from the strain, but I was afraid Vito would faint on the way home. It was torture for me to watch Vito, in agony, climb his stairs, but knowing I'm doing a good deed made me feel better. Mrs. M thinks I'm so wonderful, "especially for a rich person." I really should write up Vito's recent medical history & send it to Geraldo Rivera or someone.

I'm going to watch the Canadian election returns now.

Sunday, July 9, 1972

I just got home after getting some groceries at Publix, and everyone must have gone to the beach or someplace.

We all went to the Diplomat at 10 AM for the Youth Caucus. There were about 50 delegates under 30 from N.Y., but the whole thing seemed sort of silly. There's a Women's Caucus and a Gay Caucus and Black, Latino and Jewish Caucuses. I made a joke about everyone being the Captive of the Caucuses (Caucasus) to Leon, figuring he might get it because he's going to grad school in Comp Lit. But he just looked at me blankly, so I don't think he's read Andrei Bitov. Mikey just sat there saying nothing, and seeing how other people like Mike Gerstein sounded, I think he did the right thing.

In the lobby, I ran into Rob, who took me to see Liz Holtzman, who I guess is looking for a Congressional staff since she won the primary against Manny Celler. I can't imagine what she'll look like if she serves 50 years in the House like he did. The big thing, Liz said, is the seating of the Calif. delegation – if McGovern gets all the delegates, he's got the nomination. But isn't it kind of hypocritical to rely on the state's winner-take-all primary rules when he chaired the committee to reform the process?

It took a long time for all the 278 state delegates to caucus. There's a fight for the chairmanship of the N.Y. delegation between Joe Crangle, the state chairman; Mary Ann Krupsak, an upstate legislator; and Bronx Boro Pres. Bob Abrams. Mayor Lindsay looked tanned and handsome, as usual the Golden Boy even if he did horrible in the primaries; Bella Abzug was in a feisty mood and a floppy hat; the Queens boss Marty Troy dressed like a slob; and sanitation commish Jerry Kretchmer wore a T-shirt. I also spotted Al Lowenstein, Herman Badillo, and Arthur Schlesinger in his bow tie. There was a minor revolt as the diehard reformers tried to oust Crangle from the Rules Committee, but he survived.

Mikey and I had lunch in the coffee shop, then I went with Leon and Skip down Collins Ave. to the candidates' HQ at the various hotels. We collected lots of buttons and posters from the campaigns of Muskie, Humphrey, and Chisholm, and we put this big poster, "Wilbur Mills for President," with his big red nose, on the hood of the Pontiac. At the Doral, Skip tried to say, "We're with Mills," but I don't think they believed we were workers for the chairman of the, as it's always called, "powerful Ways and Means Committee."

We were trying to find Gene McCarthy HQ, but the people at the hotel where it was supposed to be said they'd never even heard of him. We also went to the HQ of the two idiotic Vice Presidential candidates, Alaska Sen. Mike Gravel (who I actually shook hands with) and former Mass. Gov. Endicott "Chub" Peabody. (There's a joke in Updike's *Couples*: Q: What three cities in Mass. are named for him? A: Endicott, Peabody, and Marblehead.)

Then there was a cocktail party for the N.Y. delegation back at the Diplomat, but they served just watery punch and stale pretzels, not real cocktails. They turned the cameras on only when Big John came in to mingle. I went up to Mary Lindsay and started telling her I first met her when I was only 14 and they were campaigning on the beach at Rockaway, but she simply nodded and smiled.

The atmosphere in this town is absurd. The Zippies and others are downtown camping out in Flamingo Park, and the Convention Hall has barbed wire around it.

Thursday, July 10, 1973

I spoke to Gary late last night & we had a talk unlike most of those we've been having lately. It was not superficial in that Gary mentioned for the first time his feelings about Hilda. For months, they've been so much a couple that one hardly thought of them as individuals. Every time I saw Gary he was always with Hilda, on his way to seeing her, or just returning from seeing her. But apparently there have been some problems.

"It's all been downhill since March," Gary said. Curious how it dates from their acceptances at Columbia. Hilda says that Gary resents her getting him in with the Soc. Dep't, getting him to switch his major & helping getting him into grad school at Columbia. Hilda says that Gary's been "bitchy" & he denies it. They've leaving for Europe next week, & Gary hopes the trip will bring them closer together again.

Gary also mentioned speaking to Kjell & that Sharon is indeed due this week. They hope for a natural, not a Caesarean, birth.

On my breakfast table this morning, I saw Ivan's sister's photo again on page 4 of the News with a headline, "Many a Guy Dials Page 1 Gal." The article mentioned how after "Mona's now-famous dash through the Rockaway surf," everyone with her last name got calls for her yesterday. It broke the "disappointing" news that Mona's a Mrs. & went on to catalogue her food tastes, her interest in yoga & her dog Cinnamon. From clothing manufacturer's daughter to sex symbol overnight.

At BC, I showed the paper to Mavis & Susan, to whom I'd pointed out Mona on the beach last Friday. Vito said, "You just *know* she's going to get a movie contract!" Vito, Mavis & I went for lunch & noted that Vito is stuffing himself again - I counted 5 cups of Italian ices. I told Mavis that I liked Bob & urged her to keep seeing him despite his other girlfriend. Vito commented that people usually think the worst & mentioned how many people think Mavis & I are having an affair because we hang around a lot together, or the rumors about him & Tony, who has a girlfriend after all.

On my way to my car, I ran into Stacy, who was exceedingly friendly, which pleased me. She's having a relationship, but the guy is up in Syracuse, unfortunately. She's still hoping to get to California this summer, but is meanwhile coordinating Scholar's Program theses in the School of Social Science. I wished her luck - sincerely, I might add - & then went to Richmond to be bored by Prof. Cullen's last lecture on Victorian prose.

I wrote to Mansarde, inviting her & Christine to stay with us - I doubt they'll accept, but it would be fun if they did. It clouded up & may storm tonight. This is going to be a rough week - a lot of work.

Saturday, July 11, 1970

A hot, humid day. Jonny was up early & went for drum lessons. Marc & I woke later & together we went to the Brook to see "Boys in the Band." It depressed him altho he admitted it was great, & I have to confess I didn't come out of the theater feeling very happy, either. We got home at 3:30 & I went out back to read Twain's "The Mysterious Stranger," which Mark has been nagging me to do.

Gary called his mother this morning, very upset. He was recycled to a special training unit. I guess they think he's trying to get out, so now he's on rigorous discipline: 8 hours a day of physical training, daily inspection, no packages. His mother worried that now he may not be able to go to school in Sept. I'm going to look in on her.

We got a call from Rose & Lou Gross in London. Their son David's been here for 2 weeks & they have no word from him. His tour group checked out of the McAlpin, & all they have is this Kane St. address where they send his mail.

Grandma Sylvia's & Grandpa Nat's 50th anniversary party was tonight at Carl Hoppl's in Baldwin. The family went, but I stayed home. I hate those things worse than the plague. Maybe it's my neurosis, but I just don't believe in doing things I don't enjoy. I hope Grandma & Grandpa don't take offense.

Anyway, I had a nice evening. I went out to Wollman Rink & watched the young troupe rehearse a play, "Now We Are Free." They're very good. Still, I wish I was a participant rather than sitting on the sidelines.

Sunday, July 12, 1970

A day concerned with other people's problems. The party last night was enjoyable, my parents said, altho I'm glad I didn't go. This morning I drove to the Kane St. address that David gave as his mailing address. I found a letter for him in the hall (from the tour group, asking him to contact his parents). There were also messages for him to pick up telegrams under the name David Gross Chez. No one in the building is named Chez, but I called a Mrs. Scott who was going to ask all the tenants if they know anything. She called me tonight: no luck. Curiouser & curiouser.

Gary's parents, his uncle Izzy & Gary's friend Sidney & I had a long conference about Gary in the Milsteins' ap't. He's sick, depressed & is at the end of his wits. He called later & said he's going to try to pass the PT tests & seemed to cheer up a bit. Sidney said we should stop letting Gary play on our sympathy & Mr. M said we should pull no punches. Mrs. M is very upset & wanted me to write a letter to the chaplain, but the men thought it's best to let things be.

From there I had lunch & went to a party given by the Committee to Defend the Panthers. All my favorite radicals were there - Li, Cliff, Kenny, LeRoy, Lou, Iggy. I gave a contribution & we listened to Dylan & a Cleaver speech.

I went to the Cohens tonight to see if they had any

idea about David G. They said he's probably just irresponsible. I think that's awful, as the Gs are worried sick in London. How can others depend upon me when I'm so undependable?

Tuesday, July 13, 1971

One of those days when nothing really goes right. I hardly slept last night - I was having nightmares & my legs ached & my stomach hurt. I went to school & talked with Red, who's going to study in Spain next year. Avis joined me & we went to the steps of LaGuardia, where Elspeth was burning a candle she'd made. Alice came along & the four of us sat transfixed, watching the candle drip over the steps. Elspeth said we should sacrifice a virgin but I looked around at her, Alice & Avis & said I didn't think we could find one. A couple of Wackenhuts arrived & made us put it out. Lighting candles is probably a violation of the Henderson Rules.

In Poli Sci, Prof. Gluck said he'd give me an A & I didn't even need to hand in the last paper, so I did that work for nothing. After class, I met Shelli on the steps & demonstrated some yoga for her & Slade. Charles came by & we walked him to his Cougar. We all drove down Flatbush Ave. & had lunch at the Floridian. Charles is going to Madison next week to check out the University of Wisconsin grad school, & he's leaving for Europe soon after. Charles got a letter from Leon, who was in Italy & heading for

Yugoslavia. Charles also got a call from Gary. All Gary talked about was the Guard, Charles said.

The three of us came to my house & Charles was going to show Jonny how to play stickball. Jonny hit 3 balls in a row & then Charles got 7 strikes in a row, after which he went home to study for his final. Shelli & I sat around for a while, talking with Grandpa Herb & Grandma Ethel, who came over while their car was being fixed at Bob's. Shelli had to read, so I drove her to the college, stopping on the way to drop Grandma & Grandpa off to see "Love Story" at Kings Plaza.

I took a nap & read the rest of the boring afternoon. My phone fell & broke but our neighbor J.B., who works for the phone company, graciously fixed it. I tried to call Gary, but his mother said he went out with Sidney somewhere.

Monday, July 14, 1975

While washing my face just now, my reflection in the mirror looked handsome. Of course I didn't have my glasses on. This evening I went over to Josh's to see him before he takes off for California on Wednesday. Driving around while looking for a parking space, I saw this teenage girl walking around with the best set of breasts I've seen in a long time. She was wearing a danskin, which is enough to drive me crazy anyway (I think women look their best in danskins), but her breasts seemed almost perfect: round, high & firm.

"I'm in love," I said dreamily to Josh as I entered his apartment. He knew the girl I was speaking of; she lives upstairs from him. He & Keith are taking a noon flight to San Francisco on Wednesday; first they're going to stay at this woman's place in Santa Cruz. Josh said he may spend a half-hour or two weeks there. The woman sounds adorable from Josh's description, if slightly fucked-up (but who isn't?). She doesn't like guys to come in her mouth, but I can't blame her for that.

Josh's friend Fat Ronnie, of whom he's spoken often, arrived straight from work at Starrett City, the new housing project near the Belt Parkway. Fat Ronnie dropped out of college & is doing construction work there - his father is vice president of the company & got him the job. While Josh was cooking the spaghetti for their dinner (I had eaten at home: Mom's pepper steak), Fat Ronnie took out some hash & we smoked - he & I did anyway; Josh always abstains. Josh & Fat Ronnie must be friends for a long time, as Fat Ronnie knows Vinnie, who hasn't spoken to Josh in a month. Leslie is the reason Vinnie's mad at Josh. Remember that day when I ran into him in the rain & drove him to Leslie's apartment? Well, Vinnie heard about it & got the wrong idea.) Fat Ronnie, who seems like a real nice guy, wants to move to California & set up some kind of business there, a business where he doesn't have to work too hard & which will enable him to live as he chooses. I must have gotten a bit stoned, because when Fat Ronnie said the phrase "...to live as

I choose," I thought he said "...to live as a Jew."

Anyway, I left at about 10 PM, telling Josh to have a great time out on the Coast; the only thing that might upset him is that he's going to pick up his sister's belongings. But he should have a good time - he won't be back until the second week of September.

I woke up early this morning, feeling pressure in my sinuses. It's like monsoon season here, with rain every day & flash floods in the Jersey suburbs. I made the now-familiar trek to 42nd Street & arrived early, as usual. Miss Belfer is going very quickly - today we did a lot of translating & went over all the compound tenses. I enjoy our breaks in the cafeteria. Today Miss Belfer talked about sitting in the bar of the Raleigh Hotel when some doofus file clerk for the Welfare Dep't came over and asked for her number. She told him that she moves around a lot & that she'd better take *his* number instead.

I came home at 2PM, & after lunch I worked for over an hour on my homework, translating the first chapter of *Candide*. I enjoy having some fluidity in French, & oddly enough, after over 7 years, my high-school Spanish is coming back. Marc has been feeling better & he went over to visit Marilyn today. Mom was upset that he was gone so long on such a miserable day & by the fact that he was probably kissing Marilyn & possibly reinfecting himself.

I ran into Harvey today & waved to him; he gave me a 'hello' & somewhat suspicious look. I feel awkward with him, knowing how chummy he is with Ronna. Or, I should say, knowing how *close* he is with Ronna. It's not the extent of their romantic relationship, if any, that bothers me; it's the possibility that Ronna may often confide in him about me & that maybe he knows why Ronna is angry with me. It's been 4 whole weeks since I last spoke to Ronna.

Saturday, July 15, 1972

It's now Saturday night, 9PM, & I'm home, in bed, exhausted yet exhilarated. I know I've just gone through one of the most meaningful experience of my life, the trip to Miami for the Convention. I am glad I went & always shall be. I didn't need my mommy and daddy to hold my hand through this experience; I had some panic attacks this past week, but I came out okay, and Leon, Skip, Mikey and I became a really tight unit. I learned a lot about living with people other than my family. I slept in the same bed as Mikey, ate off the same plate as Skip, and smoked the same joint as Leon. Wait, I've done that last thing a lot before this week.

Thursday night at the convention was a long one. The vice-presidential balloting was the most entertaining part of the convention. Although of course Eagleton won, votes were cast for Peabody and Gravel, Hodding Carter and Cissy Farenthold, and such lesser political lights as Roger Mudd, Bear Bryant, Lauren Bacall, Father Berrigan, Martha Mitchell, and Jerry Rubin. Mikey voted, God bless him, for Abe Ribicoff. But the hijinks went on for such a long time, it was incredibly late when McGovern got to give his acceptance speech. The theme was "Come home, America," and it was great, but I think most people, even on the West Coast, were probably asleep because it ended at 3 a.m., midnight Pacific time.

On Friday we awoke at 11 a.m. and closed up the condominium, taking our stuff out. We stopped off downtown to say goodbye to Leon's Uncle Max and Aunt Leah, who seem sweet and are so poor they don't even have air-conditioning. Then we watched the Zippies and other kids leaving their campground in Flamingo Park, backpacks on, hitching north or west.

We started driving at 1 p.m., stopped for lunch and for Skip to throw up (I'm the only one of the four of us who didn't vomit on this trip) and to buy oranges, jellies, and Florida souvenirs. We weren't making very good time when, as Mikey was driving at 80 m.p.h., we had a blowout near Cape Kennedy. We changed it, but the spare was no good, so we had to drive to Merritt Island to buy a new one. Luckily I had Milt Littman's $50.

After dinner in Titusville, we kept driving, driving, driving through the night. Skip drove mostly, and

Leon kept putting food in Skip's mouth to keep him awake. At about 4 a.m., Skip couldn't go on, and we pulled over into a rest area. A few hours later we woke up all sore from sleeping in strange positions in a cramped car.

I got very dizzy while I was driving around Richmond. I thought I was going to pass out, and I called Shelley Wouk from a phone booth to talk to her for a while. Reassured, I set out again. Skip decided to get off at Arlington to visit his bewildered fascist parents. The Ds are a big military family, so you understand how they feel about a son like Skip, a radical long-haired faggot.

In one of my few serious talks with Skip – his name suits him so, as he's hardly ever not smiling – I learned how hard it was on him being gay and yet getting coerced into being a big jock and enlisting in the Navy for Vietnam. He never talks about what happened to him in the war, but I heard that his ship was bombed and he was the last person to get down the stairs or whatever they call them, and that all the guys who came after him died.

We stopped in Bethesda, on Wisconsin Ave., for something to eat, and I dropped by to see Sid B at his carpet store. Then Leon, Mikey and I drove back to N.Y. It was great to see the Belt Parkway again even though it was the only traffic jam we had on the whole trip back. Around 7 p.m. we arrived in

Rockaway, where Mrs. V and all the neighbors on Beach 128th St. greeted us like conquering heroes.

While I was on the phone telling Grandpa Nat and Grandma Sylvia I'd arrived back home, I noticed a phone message from Shelli. Mrs. V said Shelli had called, asking when "the boys" would be home and could they come to a party she and Jerry were giving to celebrate the convention. I wondered if that invitation included me.

When I dropped Leon off at his house on Snyder Ave., he said that now, with another burst of energy, I could continue and drive up the 100 miles to my parents' hotel in South Fallsburg. But I wanted to go back to East 56th St.

Later Shelli called, saying Leon was at their party and telling everyone about the convention and saying they'd like to see me too. Did the "they" mean her and her husband? It would be freaky to go to their house, but I'm too tired anyway. I feel like I'm still going 70 m.p.h. and I really feel funky after riding in a car for more than 24 hours.

It's a long time till November and this young Democrat needs a bath.

Monday, July 16, 1973

It's only 7PM, but I'm extremely tired. I spent an almost sleepless night tossing & turning in bed. Nothing is bothering me - at least not enough to keep me awake for that long a period of time, but I was without my tranquilizers, which usually give me relief from sleeplessness. Insomnia is a great equalizer. When it's 4 or 5 AM & you're still awake, it's as tho your present day-to-day reality means nothing: you could be 17 years old or 12, or 6. Needless to say, I felt so rotten upon awakening from just a 2-hour sleep, I decided not to go to school today. The car was being worked on at the body shop anyway, & I guess I can afford to miss one class.

I got a letter today from Avis, from San Diego. She seems to be enjoying herself immensely, going up & down the coast from San Francisco to Disneyland to Tijuana. Libby, she writes, "is the sweetest & loveliest person," but Bev has been "cramping our style" altho their days are still busy & fun-filled.

Gary called last night; he'd gone to Great Neck for the weekend to think things thru. There's absolutely no doubt that he & Hilda are finished. On Friday there was a "virtual war" in the office & that night he went over to his house to retrieve his belongings. (An ancient ritual, Ronna & I recalled: Shelli's bathing suits & my St. Christopher's medal were returned;

Ivan's shorts & Ronna's copy of *Love Story* were never given back.)

Hilda has turned very cold toward Gary & he dreads the hassles he may have to face in Columbia, seeing her so often. Gary will probably go away, alone perhaps. He doesn't feel like seeing people yet - prospective girlfriends, anyway. I don't think they're going to reconcile; Gary says he's run after her twice already & altho he may still love her, it's not worth it.

It's amazing the way people's feelings about their lovers change. Perhaps they were victims of a stifling, clutching love as Shelli & I were. Ronna said that on Saturday night Jerry kept hugging & kissing Shelli in public & it embarrassed her. But who knows? Ivan's father once said he couldn't imagine whatever Ivan saw in Ronna. "But, Daddy, I *love* her," Ivan said. Maybe it's that simple - I don't know.

I went over to see Mrs. W today & she said Sharon's overdue & very uncomfortable. Kjell's tense & she (Mrs. W) can't leave the house since she's always waiting for Sharon to call to ask her to take her to the hospital. "You're a good mother-in-law," I told Mrs. W.

Wednesday, July 17, 1974

Late yesterday afternoon, I went to the Junction to buy Dad a birthday card. Brendan, whom I met at

Libby's house, was working the cash register & we
chatted for a while. He asked how my thesis is going
(answer: it's going nowhere at the moment) & said
he'll be leaving for Maine soon, to that beach house
that he so obviously loves.

I spotted Barbara's friend Tom going out of the
subway & caught up with him. He was coming from
his new job at Warner Bros. in Manhattan & had to
eat before a 6PM class, so I joined him in McDonald's.
We talked so much, discovering that we have a lot in
common: he has sinusitis, liked "Cries & Whispers" &
"Discreet Charm of the Bourgeoisie." He said he
probably could use a shrink although he plays the
role of a neurotic with gusto. I can tell he's
homosexual - his speech & mannerisms are vaguely
effeminate & he has that sense of humor that gay
people like Stephen & Teresa's friend Jesse have. Tom
said he liked me a lot & I found him to be a really nice
& funny person. I walked Tom to class - he said most
of his friends are still from high school, that he hasn't
met anyone in college.

Driving around, I spotted Melvin walking in my
neighborhood & dropped him off at his parents'
house. He was going to give them a thrill by popping
in, he said. Melvin's working, mostly; he thought he
could make up his incompletes this summer but he
just can't work it in, so he'll graduate in January. I told
him to tell his brother I'd return the book I borrowed
& then let him go. Melvin still always looks like

someone just woke him out of a sound sleep.

I headed for Rockaway (when I told Melvin where I was going, he almost changed his mind about going to his parents & said, "It's so beautiful at the beach"). I found Grandpa Herb & Grandma Ethel on the boardwalk & I joined them on their bench overlooking the ocean. Grandma Ethel said that dusk is her favorite part of the day. It was so mild, we stayed there until it became dark, watching the surfers & seagulls. I went home soon after, wished Ronna good luck on her finals, & went to bed.

I was restless this morning, worried about Grandma Sylvia's operation. So I decided to drive up to New York Hospital; even tho I couldn't do anything, I wanted to be around. Does that make sense? I know the operation was a long procedure & I was quite anxious. I finally found the right building (Special Surgery) & inquired about Grandma at the desk. The nurse called up & told me that surgery had been successful, the operation was over, but Grandma would be in the Recovery Room overnight.

I felt better, & after calling Grandpa Nat at "the place" to confirm the good news, I went up a few blocks to the BHE Annex. Ira sent me some Chancellor's Committee material & enclosed a note saying he'd been trying to reach me, so I thought I'd visit him at the University Student Senate office. Ira wasn't there when I arrived; however, Clay & Mary invited me to come to have lunch with them. It was nice to be invited; they jokingly told me about getting drunk & having a late-night card game last night with Ira & Dewayne. At another table, I spotted Duncan Pardue with Vice-Chancellor Healy - he's University Public Relations Director now. I remember him when he did the same thing at BC. Clay said that Dean Gedney is gone now & they're searching for a replacement. When Ira arrived, he told me to sit in on the Steering Committee meeting with him & look over some resumes of people who had applied for the Executive Director's job. Steve & Wes were also there. I didn't find any suitable applicants, tho I saw that Avi submitted a resume.

Wednesday, July 18, 1973

It's early evening & I feel a little sad. I'm almost lonely, tho I have no lack of people to talk to & do things with. Even tho Mom & Dad are away (& perhaps that foreshadows the fears I have of leaving home), there are still dozens of people I can rely on, not the least of whom is Ronna. But still there's that uneasy feeling - it's a throwback to something in the past, something half-forgotten. Or perhaps I *enjoy* the feeling.

Ronna & I saw "Slaughterhouse-Five" last night, where the Tralfamadorian tells Billy Pilgrim, "A pleasant way to spend eternity is to concentrate on the good moments and forget the bad ones." It sounds fine, but the bad moments can keep recurring out of habit, & maybe the reason I'm in therapy is to get at those bad moments, the first ones - but there'll always be bad moments, anyway. So remembering the good: I picked up Ronna at 7:30 last night, & she was punctual & looked terrific.

We went to the Quad in the city, & Ronna enjoyed the film. She's tired of working at the insurance company, but they would like to keep her on for the whole summer. It was an entirely pleasant evening - Ronna & I are close, & I think that's great.

Marc drove the rest of the family to the airport, & I had nothing to do, so I went to BC. It may be immature for me to keep going back, but at least on campus there are always people to see: Liz, working at the day-care center, & Allan, Mike & Lee. I saw Hilda & she waved to me - I guess she must feel awkward. I hung around for a long time with Vito & Mavis - the three of us are almost a unit. Vito told me how he went to the GAA Firehouse with Joe & they met Skip, John & a whole Bklyn College contingent there.

I ran into Barry, whom I've been avoiding every time he calls my house - I just don't feel like getting involved with his craziness. But I was glad to come across Josh in the library. We went to lunch at Jentz's. He's getting around okay despite his mono, altho he can't kiss anyone & still is the cynic, trying to outwit teachers & find relief from life's boredom. I missed talking with him, altho he does have the annoying habit of asking questions like "Why aren't you having an affair with Mavis?" - to which I sputter some feeble response. But Josh's a good kid.

Sunday, July 19, 1970

Last night's fever went down as I took a bath - it must have been too much sun. I had a restless night & felt icky this morning. In the Times, Laurence Luckenbill, who played Hank in "Boys in the Band," wrote an interesting article how actors are irrelevant. I drove downtown & to the Heights, taking pictures of the Slack Bar, Meyer Levin junior high & our old house.

When I arrived home, Uncle Marty & Aunt Arlyne were already here, at the pool. Joey has picked up a few new words but still doesn't talk much. They're all going to visit Wendy at camp on Thursday. Uncle Marty has grown a Fu Manchu mustache. We had a barbecue & I talked with Aunt Arlyne, who may be going back to college.

After they left, I went to the park again to see the one show I missed of the four plays in repertory. It was "The People vs. Ranchman" by Megan Terry, pretty good. Later, for English I tried to understand an Adrienne Kennedy play, "A Rat's Mass." I don't know why I find it so difficult to comprehend these things - I'm not exactly thick.

Mom & Dad are preparing for their trip to Las Vegas Wednesday. They're going with the Cohens & others - unfortunately, the Bernsteins will be staying at the same hotel.

Monday, July 20, 1970

A humid, hazy day - it started storming tonight. Kjell & I went to school together. I wanted to invite him & his girlfriend over this Sunday but forgot to ask him. In Speech we started the speeches to convince - I think I'm going to do mine on the seniority system in Congress. In English, Mr. Graves cleared up some of the points in "A Rat's Mass." He gave back last week's essays, & I was surprised to get a B+.

I went into the office & talked to Mark for a while. Somehow I don't think he believes half the things I tell him. I had lunch, & then went downtown to see Dr. Wouk. He's leaving tomorrow for a lecture tour of Europe & will be back in six weeks. He said he got a different impression of my parents from their visit than I gave him - Dad, especially. We discussed Mansarde's visit, my plans for the rest of the summer & other junk. I'm going to miss Dr. Wouk.

Grandpa Herbie is on vacation this week, so I passed by the store. At home, I looked thru my mail - I received the election laws of Colo. & Mass. Also the application from Joseph Whitehill, the director of

Mensa Friends. I filled it out & now hope they'll send me the name of a prison inmate I can correspond with. It should prove interesting - maybe I can help someone & make a friend.

Tonight I got out some library books on population & birth control. I watched some TV & saw two people I admire, Dick Gregory & Pete Seeger. It's been a year since the moon landing, & nothing terribly wonderful has happened since then.

Wednesday, July 21, 1971

A nice sort of lazy day. I had a nightmare early this morning & in my sleep I knocked over my nighttable, waking the whole house. Dad took off work today to celebrate his 45th birthday. The first fruits of my mailing away for stuff came today: a game called Who Can Beat Nixon?, which is very cute. I also got a letter from Shelli's sister, who gave me the names of several good (& bad) English teachers. They've moved into their apartment in Seattle, but she's terribly disappointed that she didn't make law school.

I went to Shelli's house at 11AM. She's been wearing makeup lately & looks really nice & feminine. We drove to the Brooklyn Museum, which is in financial trouble - they had to cut back hours. We looked at an exhibition of Russian art of the Revolution & a show of emotionally disturbed children's art. Then we bought some things at the Gallery Shop & walked thru the sculpture garden. We stopped back at her house & found that she'd received a bunch of books. Mrs. N, watching Shelli's grandmother, said that Shelli's friend Brian was over while we were out. Shelli later called him, & we'll see him on Friday.

Shelli & I had lunch at Georgetowne, then went home & played the Nixon game with Jonny. After it was over, Shelli & I made love. We had to make it fast, so we made love practically dressed - it was beautiful nonetheless. We went to Avis's apartment to say goodbye. She showed us her traveler's cheques & passport & gave us her mailing addresses (I noticed Elihu's bicycle in Avis's living room.) We had a nice hour of conversation, then I drove Shelli to Dr. Russell.

While she was with him, I went over to the college. In my mailbox, I found a press release announcing the school's new vice president, Sherman Van Solkema. I drove Shelli home & came back to my house. Dad took the family out tonight so I had to handle calls from Grandma Sylvia, Grandma Ethel & Aunt Sydelle, who just returned from the Catskills.

Tuesday, July 22, 1975

8 PM. I didn't get any writing today as I'd hoped to, but I was involved with *people* instead of words for a change & that did me good. I can't hermetically seal myself off from the world; I am somewhat gregarious

& need people around me. Libby called me this afternoon & asked if I could do her a big favor: go with her to a free clinic in Coney Island. I had planned to write all afternoon, but I didn't hesitate for a second before saying yes.

When I arrived at Libby's apartment, she was getting dressed & she was visibly nervous. She told me that she had never been to a gynecologist before although Avis & others had tried to get her to go, so she was very scared of the procedure. Her roommate Marisol, who was home with a cold, attempted to reassure Libby, & I of course made my old puns about the miscarriage trade & a gynecologist always being at one's cervix. At least Libby groaned & it took her mind off her anxiety.

We drove to the clinic, which was in a project in Coney Island's slums. Libby had an appointment at 3:30 PM, but the doctor didn't arrive until nearly 6 PM, as there was an emergency in Coney Island Hospital. In the time we had to wait, I held Libby's hand (literally) & tried to ease her tension. The people there were very nice; when Libby told them that it was her first time, a woman explained the whole procedure to her beforehand. Libby was sort of pale after they took 4 vials of blood, but she felt better after a while. We were practically the only white people in the clinic; there were a lot of Black & Hispanic women & children there.

I went out for a while to call the YWCA & tell them that Libby would be late for work (she teaches swimming & is a lifeguard) & to get some gas for my car. I felt a little strange waiting in the clinic, expecting someone to ask me, "Hey, man, yo' done knock up yo' fox?" or something. But I remembered the time I took Shelli to Planned Parenthood on Court St.; that was nearly 4 years ago but I remember it so clearly. We were scared kids then. I even remember I was wearing a nice grey body shirt & new jeans, jeans Shelli had bleached out for me. Shelli was wearing her purple dashiki that I liked so much, & she got her period right before the exam - we were so scared that she was pregnant. Writing that whole experience, for the first time in many years, I remember those days with fondness & poignancy.

Libby finally came out, a bit pale, & she instinctively took my hand. It was worth any inconvenience to me to feel like I was her protector. If that's male chauvinism, then I'm guilty. She has a simple infection & a discharge. She told me it was the first time a long time that she'd slept with someone besides Mason & she felt terrible about possibly giving it to Mason when he came in from camp. The doctor gave her pills for herself & for Mason, & vaginal suppositories, & he told her to douche when possible.

But the doctor also told her that she had an ovarian cyst & that she should take x-rays at Coney Island

Hospital - I don't know if that's very serious; it's possible that it might get smaller. But Libby was shaking & so I took her to The Foursome, where we could relax & have some dinner, & afterwards she felt much better. (I was surprised when Libby told me she hasn't eaten meat in 3 years.) Then we took a twilight drive along the Belt & BQE to the YWCA on Atlantic Avenue. Libby told me I was welcome to come in for a swim, but I decided I'd spend an hour with Vito, which was a treat. He's still as funny as ever, & all the reasons why I have always liked him still remain. It was great for me to feel needed today; I am so lucky.

Wednesday, July 23, 1975

7 PM. Perhaps I'm entering a fallow period with my writing; I was only able to creak out three pages yesterday, & today, nothing. I seem to be singularly uncreative these days. Last evening this guy named Felix called me. He said that he was one of 6 people accepted into the MFA program in Fiction & wanted to know something about it. Hoops had given him my number. So I went into a whole routine about the program & told him that I felt it was worthwhile, but that I felt, as with most things, that you get out when you put into it. Josh puts in nothing & gets nothing from it, while I've gotten a great deal out of the program. Along that line, I told this guy to get another opinion, so I gave him Denis' number. Felix also was accepted into the City College M.A. program, which is much bigger & boasts Joseph

Heller & Donald Barthelme, but he lives in Park Slope
& it's such a hassle to get to Harlem.

As I said, yesterday I spent some time with Vito. He's
taking an Audiology course this summer, & working
hard at it, but he isn't that happy doing graduate
work. He's still not working, but he manages to go to
all the shows & movies around town. Vito's gay, but
he's not gay in the weird way that Allan & Jerry &
Leon are gay. Vito dresses like an average Joe & he
told me that Allan "belongs to a very strange scene";
Vito is easy-going & can relate to heterosexuals better.
Like he spoke about his crush on Frank or how he
likes to look at the cute guys in *Playgirl*; if this doesn't
sound ridiculous, Vito strikes me as really
wholesome. We talked about various people: Tony
isn't friendly with him anymore & he hasn't seen Joe
for some time. He remarked how much friendlier to
him Mike & Mikey had become, & he said he saw
Debbie, whom he said "now looks good that she's put
on some weight & gotten rid of that makeup." Altho
Vito & I will never be the closest of friends, it's good
to know that we can always pick up the threads of
our relationship after long stretches apart.

I also saw Ronna's sister yesterday - or rather, she
spotted me. I gave her a friendly greeting but I didn't
ask about Ronna, & later I was glad I hadn't. I also
spoke to Gary, who said teaching is going fine & that
his parents enjoyed their trip to the Maritime
Provinces. He spent the weekend at his sister's in

New Jersey & got stuck in a lot of traffic due to the flooding that resulted from the very heavy rains; the whole state has been declared a disaster area.

And last night, Mikey called. I had driven over to his house on Sunday after leaving the beach in Neponsit, but Mikey's mother said that he was over at Larry's & I didn't feel like going over there. Mikey explained to me just whose car was in his driveway on Sunday. It seems he met this girl on the beach the previous weekend & took her number altho she wouldn't take his. He called her on Wednesday night & asked her out for Saturday. She told him she might be going to the Hamptons & to call her back later. He did, & she was still unsure. The next night he got no answer & on Friday he went to the Mets game with a neighbor & forgot about it. While he was at Larry's on Sunday, the girl came over & parked in his driveway, telling Mrs. V that she was a friend of Mikey's & he'd said she could always park there. When he finally caught up to her, she complained that she ended up sitting home alone on Saturday night. Mikey said that is the end of that relationship. Yesterday Mikey was uptown near Columbia & had to get to Lenox Ave. for a meeting about the Rikers Island program at John Jay, so he walked thru Morningside Park - & lived to tell about it.

I got very little sleep last night & had a bad sinus headache this morning, but I forced myself to go to Manhattan for class. And I'm glad I went - from now on until the end of the term, we're just doing straight translations.

Tuesday, July 24, 1973

10 PM. I arrived home just now; on the stairs I passed some of Marc's friends staggering out, totally wrecked. I'm not sure why (probably it's just a phase), but I haven't had the slightest desire to smoke grass in months. Oh, I'll get stoned at parties when everyone else is doing it & I'd even do it with a friend, but somehow it all seems silly. Perhaps I'm becoming too straight - pot is okay to relax with occasionally, but flying high is not the greatest feeling in the world.

Gary picked me up at 7 PM tonight & we went to Brookdale Hospital; he'd called me late last night with the news that Sharon had given birth. As Gary will be leaving for London tomorrow, he wanted to see her tonight & I said I'd accompany him. Sharon looked really well for a girl who'd had a very difficult Caesarean childbirth the day before. With her red hair, freckles, dressed in a pink nightgown, she looked positively beautiful. Kjell was beaming as a proud father should - he's put on weight & is not the 'rail' he's always been since P.S. 203; I guess it's Sharon's cooking. He brought her a beautiful silver heart-shaped pendant, & you could just see how in love they are.

His mother & hers took Gary & me to see their

granddaughter thru the screen: Alison Meredith, 7 lbs., 6 oz. She's not pretty (I've never seen a pretty newborn baby), but it's so remarkable to see the tiny features: the ears, the fingers, all perfect. The grandmothers argued jokingly about who the baby looked more like, & all I could think of were inane clichés about "the miracle of life." But it's such a responsibility: it's not a possession, it's a separate human being. Still, I think Sharon & Kjell will be good, loving parents.

Gary dropped me off at my house & I wished him a very good vacation. He's finally getting to go to Europe & I hope it turns out well for him, with all the bad breaks he's had lately.

This morning I sat outside listening to the Watergate hearings, the new TV sensation - but surprisingly, it *is* fascinating as well as important. In class today, Prof. Cullen began Browning - there's no class tomorrow, & in 2 weeks the course will have ended.

Ronna was afraid of offending Felicia & Susan, whom she had originally offered to see "Streetcar" with us, & didn't tell them we'd already seen it. So where is Ms. Ronna tonight? Seeing "Streetcar" & making believe she's doing it for the first time. What a comedy.

Tuesday, July 25, 1972

I awoke early this morning from an incredible dream, now mostly forgotten, about being in prison. As soon as Maud came in, I took the car & drove off into the city. I parked on 8th St. in the Village & took a walk around. The Village seems seedier & a less joyous place than it was when I first discovered it three years ago. There were kids in the fountain in Washington Square, but the people around seemed detached & hostile; perhaps they're frightened. I spotted this one kid, a boy about 16, barechested with a beautiful muscular body & long wavy brown hair; he looked incredibly sexy & he looked so sure of his sexuality. I couldn't help staring at him with a mixture of envy & lust. I couldn't keep my eyes off him - just like *Death in Venice*. It upset me a little - I must discuss it with Shelley Wouk.

In Marboro Books, I bought 2 Vonnegut novels, reduced to $1. Then I walked thru Azuma & the Postermat & hung around the Electric Circus, but it all seemed so forlorn compared to 1969. Before going back to B'klyn, I drove by Madison Square Garden - cops were everywhere, ready for the Stones concert tonight.

I went to the college, &, lonely for company, offered to buy Paul lunch. He accepted. Paul is into so many things, all of them half-assed. Paul - or "Pablo," as the Third Worlders call him - asked me I wanted to be a delegate to the NSA's National Student Congress, held in Washington next month. I said yes - I'd love to spend a week in the capital - but I doubt it will come off. I have the feeling Paul has a crush on Skip - he keeps talking about him. In any case, I think Paul is very immature. While were in the student gov't office, Dean McGee came in & asked me if I, as the Election Commissioner, would file a complaint against those students who voted twice. I politely told him I wouldn't, & he said, "Think about it." I certainly won't - among the students on the list were Debbie, Mike, Barry, Shira & Ira. I saw Hal - his brother Bob's at Harvard summer school & Hal is going up to visit him tom'w. Gary & Barry were over while I was out & invited me to join them at the beach & then a movie.

Friday, July 26, 1974

I just lowered the sound on the TV: the Judiciary Committee is debating various articles of impeachment. Different ploys, amendments & arguments are being tossed about, & it doesn't look like they'll come to a vote today.

Last night I fell asleep reading *Fear of Flying*. I like the way Erica Jong writes, but she raises an interesting point: if no fiction can compare with life in complexity, no characters can compare with real people, no plot - however confused - can compare with life's "plot"...then why bother with fiction at all, except to protect the author's good name? I now intend to write "truthfully," out of my own experience only - altho Peter Spielberg feels that's when authors tend to lie the most.

Anyway, a lot of stray thoughts & feeling have been surfacing lately. Last night, in a half-asleep state, I had this vision of Jerry & Shelli as my parents, celebrating their 25th anniversary. The scene gave me a jolt & I wondered for a moment if in a sense if I didn't make them into my parents - the old Oedipus game (is that why I never slept with Shelli again after learning that Jerry fucked her?) - & I could get angry at them in a way I never could with my real parents. Also, I thought of Ivan's similarity to my father; they both have that dark big-nosed Semitic handsomeness, extreme social poise, an interest in good clothes & quality products of any kind. And in another dream, Ivan was married to Mom. Could some of my guilt & anger towards Ivan be left over from, as they say, 'an unresolved Oedipal situation' - & maybe that even made Ronna more attractive to me.

Speaking of Ronna, I went to dinner at her house last evening. She prepared veal parmigiana, spaghetti & salad for dinner, & it was very good. I enjoyed it a lot, but to my embarrassment, I had an attack of diarrhea almost immediately following dinner. It was soon over, however (& I felt relieved to learn that her brother had the same exact symptoms after eating).

We drove to Manhattan Beach when it was dark & we

walked along the bay, crossing the foot bridge on
Ocean Ave., looking at the people fishing & the boats
& smelling the sea air. We sat down on a bench on
Oriental Blv'd & necked furiously. It was exciting to
do it in public, outdoors, for once - I think Ronna
found my aggressiveness surprising but she
responded with passion. She has the best tasting lips
I've ever known (not that I'm an expert).

We returned to her house, where we did an interview
for her mother & parted at midnight. It's going to be
lonely without Ronna, but there'll be the novelty of
writing letters to each other.

I visited Mikey today & we sat on the porch; it was
cool & hazy. I asked him how his job was going & he
laughed the way people sometimes do when they're
feeling something deeply & said, "I hate it so much!"
His course at Queensborough is ending, & Mikey
seems to be bored & tired from work. But he does
have a girl he's thinking of asking out: a 25-year-old
teacher whose parents rent a bungalow on his block.
He said first he has to think of someplace good to go
to with her. Mikey's mother showed me her new
Vitamin B6/Kelp/Lecithin/Cider Vinegar diet pills.
Mikey's grandmother looks like death. Mikey told me
that Marty & Rose are having a party tom'w night &
perhaps I'll go since they told him to invite me. I
inquired about various people, & Mikey said Rob
enjoyed Bolivia despite a hassle with the secret police,
who thought he was smuggling money out of the

country; Rob's now working at a Vermont camp. Charles is excited about moving next week, & Leon may return to New York & possibly unravel the mystery of what he's been up to.

Monday, July 27, 1970

Another hot & humid day with heavy air pollution. I met Mom in the hall this morning. Their vacation was overshadowed by a near-tragedy the first night in Las Vegas. Dr. H, one of their friends, had a massive coronary in the casino. He just barely hung onto life, & they all spent a lot of time in the hospital.

Kjell told me this morning that he was going to be sworn in to the Reserves today at Ft. Tilden. I hope he has better luck than Gary has with the Nat'l Guard.

We had a discussion on advertising in Speech - kids were praising me for Friday's group. In English, Mr. Graves discussed Blake's "Marriage of Heaven & Hell" & he gave back last week's test - I got a B. It was so hot, I took off after class & came home.

I went for a hairstyling this afternoon. There was a long wait, so I went into the living room where Joe Pepitone was giving an interview to a lady reporter. He left the Houston Astros last week & there's been a big hubbub about it. I realized that he loves his image as a "bad guy." He has a serious side too, & I liked him more than before but still think he's a little odd.

Pepitone says he won't live till 40. Lennie gave me a nice styling & it was relaxing.

There was another car accident on the corner: one car went up on the Cohens' lawn & ruined Irma's bushes. We got a card from Debby from San Francisco, where she's having a good time. It's good to have Mom & Dad back again, surprisingly. There's a new American peace plan for the Middle East.

Wednesday, July 28, 1971

A mild, sunny day. I was awakened at 9 AM by a phone call from Shelli. She decided to go into Manhattan today to buy an exercise book she's been wanting, so we didn't see each other today. I spent a relaxed morning & went to the college. I was talking with Robert, Laura & Stanley about the newly named Chancellor of CUNY, Robert Kibbee - no one knows much about him except that he's Guy Kibbee's son. Elspeth told me more about Elihu's letter to Leon. Apparently it was a long denunciation & Elihu went so far as to accuse Leon & Harvey of having a perverse relationship. Leon showed the letter to Harvey, who said that Elihu must've gotten drunk one night.

Art was really fantastic: all Gauguin & Seurat. Mr. Viola is really very good. I walked with Rose to the Junction, & she said Marty's working as a camp counselor. Apparently all the political jobs he & Keith expected fell through. I took a taxi to Dr. Fletcher's office. He said that my health was generally excellent, my blood pressure & heartbeat strong. The whole thing is probably sinusitis, he diagnosed, & he gave me a prescription for antihistamines.

I spent the afternoon in the public library & doing some reading in Art. I sat out on the porch with the Wagners & the other neighbors. I noticed Mrs. Pollack's nephew is staying with her, & Edie said he would like to meet a girl. Maybe I should introduce him to Wendy; altho I've never talked with him, he seems nice & maybe he'd like Wendy. It would be safer for her than cruising Kings Highway & better on her ego: one guy she met last week wanted her to make it with his Great Dane.

Shelli called from home after her last app't for the summer with Dr. Russell. She's been on the Stillman diet all week & has lost 10 pounds. Shelli put her sister in tears last night over the phone, chewing her out for not writing. I think she's going to go out with Saul if he calls her. But I'm not that upset. She & I are getting along fine now. I just wrote a letter to Leon.

Monday, July 29, 1974

The Judiciary Committee is now debating the second article of impeachment, abuse of power, & will vote on it within the hour. The first article, on obstruction of justice, passed 27-11 Saturday night.

Six Republicans joined all the Democrats & now impeachment by the full House is all but certain.

Ronna should be in Gloucester by now - I wonder how her trip there went. Her grandmother drove her to Susan's house in Manhattan soon after I left, & early this morning they took the train to Massachusetts. I miss her a little already. Yesterday Ivan asked me if Ronna was camping out. I shrugged my shoulders & Lisa smilingly said, "You'd better check up on her." The hint being that Ronna might do something I might not approve of: this I need from Ronna's ex-boyfriend's girlfriend? But I like Lisa a lot. Ronna said she was "a doll" (she & Ivan met Lisa when Ivan was taking the bus to camp with her). I've had fantasies before of knowing Lisa, & now I have - it puts her in a frame of reference that is reality & now I don't have to wonder what she's like anymore.

But back to Ronna: Did I deliberately not pay attention to her plans in order to virtually deny the fact of her trip altogether? We had such a trauma after her trip to Cape Cod last year; neither of us were sure of the other's feelings. Ronna said, tho, that the separation will test our relationship to see if it's not out of habit. She brought up the example of Ivan & Lisa & their long separations. (I just realized the deeper meaning of one of many dreams I had last night. I dreamt that I was sitting in a restaurant petting furiously with Stacy. Mark was sitting opposite us, watching impassively, & I was afraid he would tell Ronna about it. Now that I see Lisa & Stacy & also Ivan & Mark have the same last names, it all makes sense. I suppose my ego would be pleased to steal Lisa from Ivan.)

I wonder if things will be different with Ronna moving into a new house. I'm so used to Ronna's present apartment, the car ride there, the 2 flights of steps, the iron gate. But this is a small change, & I have to adjust. Ronna's mother will be paying $50 less for the apartment on the other side of Flatlands Ave. than what her present landlord raised their rent to & have more room. Ronna's a bit upset. Her mom & I went into the basement to map out plans, but Ronna just stayed out back. I saw her sitting on the swing amid the high, uncut grass - looking sad. I hugged her goodbye so many times that we laughed. "We both have a lot of separation anxiety," I said. Mrs. Ehrlich will be gone after tomorrow & on Wednesday the family will be away & I'll have the house to myself.

Gary called this evening saying he'd gotten a job as a teaching assistant at Columbia - he'll get a tuition waiver & $1000. I told him I was happy for him, & in a way I am, but deep down jealousy rages. It's not a very attractive emotion, but it's there & I'm not going to deny it. I'd like a little recognition & some success for myself. I've all but given up hope on any of the stories I sent out being accepted for publication, so I'd better get to work on some more stuff. And my thesis, my thesis: I tell everyone "I'm writing my M.A. thesis" (doesn't that sound important?) but in reality I haven't touched it in weeks. What a charming charlatan I am.

Wednesday, July 30, 1975

8 PM. I did not have much time to think about Ronna's call or sort out my complicated feelings. Today was an exhausting day, spent helping another person. Cousin Robin called last night - Michael had fractured his leg in 2 places at day camp & she asked if Dad could come over in the morning & take Michael to the doctor. I volunteered to go along & it turned out I was needed.

I woke up at 6 AM , getting very little sleep, & Dad & I drove out to Queens very early. We arrived at Robin's apartment & found things in a bad way. Michael was whimpering in bed, in what seemed to be terrible pain, his leg in a temporary splint. At day camp yesterday, he tripped another boy, who fell on Michael's leg. Robin, who was at work (even tho she's sure she gave them her dentist-employer's phone number, as well as that of Dad's place), & so they just let poor Michael sit there all day, with the nurse telling him to stop crying.

Last night Robin took him to Booth Memorial Hospital, but there wasn't an orthopedist on call who could set it; they wanted him to stay overnight, but Robin didn't agree to that, so they put it in a splint &

let him go home. Neither Robin nor Michael got much sleep last night; he kept crying out, "I want to go home," not knowing where he was. It was so pathetic to see him lying in Robin's bed, unable to bear the pain, & it was frustrating to go through all the hassles of finding a doctor. Robin called her pediatrician, & she recommended an orthopedist, who told us to get Michael to his office by 11 AM. It was a long, tense wait, but getting him there was the hard part, as he screamed terribly whenever there was the slightest movement of his leg.

Dad & I managed to get him into a stroller a friend had lent Robin, & into Dad's car, but the poor kid was in agony. We couldn't even get a pair of shorts on him, such was his pain. And he winced at every bump the care went over on the drive to the doctor's office in Hollis. We carried him into the clinic screaming, & thankfully the doctor took him right away. Dad held him as the doctor applied a cast, & Michael howled in pain & fright. But it wasn't so bad; I didn't know before today how doctors put on a cast. Then they took some x-rays, & by then Michael had calmed down. While Dad & Robin were still in the office, I sat with him in the car (we'd taken him there by wheelchair) & we talked & he seemed to be in less pain.

The doctor said that he'll have to be in the cast for 6 weeks & that he's too young to use crutches, so he must stay still for some weeks with his leg elevated.

Michael reminded me of myself at that age, very scared but still cracking feeble jokes with the doctor, just what I used to do. We stopped off to get some food, got Michael into the stroller & had lunch in the ap't.

Robin went into Michael's room to get a little sleep & Dad dozed off in the living room while I lay on Robin's bed with Michael. He was a little cranky, but we watched TV for a while & he soon became as frisky as he always is, fighting me, twisting my nose, biting my thumb, etc. Robin had to buy a bedpan for him, as he couldn't go to the bathroom. I brought him some drinks & donuts & tried to keep him amused. I thought as I lay next to that beautiful 6-year-old boy that that's what love really is, when you have to take care of a sick child who needs you.

Dad & I were really needed today. Joel is in Washington, & of course none of Dad's nervous family can ever be told anything until after things are okay. Aunt Sydelle called just as we were getting Michael ready for the doctor & I had to disguise my voice & tell her she had the wrong number. It's a very difficult thing for a mother to raise a child alone.

The day seemed 5 years long - we had gone through so much. I felt bad that we left at 4 PM, but Dad & I had been there for 8 hours & we were falling apart. But poor Robin has to deal with this for weeks.

So you can see I didn't have time to think of my problems.

Tuesday, July 31, 1973

It's 5 PM, & if anything, I'm feeling even more depressed than I did yesterday. Last night I suffered with an extremely sore throat & had another virtually sleepless night. I'm certain, however, that the bad cold is merely a symptom or a manifestation of the acute depression I'm going thru. I haven't felt so down since those days back in December & January after Shelley Wouk decided to end her practice in the city or the time I broke up with Shelli. This depression is not easy to get out of - the cold makes me feel sluggish, & I don't feel like fighting it; I almost want to give in to the misery, which I suppose is the general idea. I am in genuine psychic pain with physical manifestations. I suppose it's the emptiness of my life facing me head-on.

All my friends, most of them anyway, are away. I got a card from Gary today & he's enjoying England; Mikey, Scott & Avis aren't home; Vito will be leaving for Europe on Friday; & Mavis's going to California. Of course Ronna's still around, which is a godsend. She told me last night that she won't be working after this week, & maybe she & I can get away in August - to Washington or Cape Cod or Florida.

I didn't go to school today, which was probably a

mistake, & I have not done any work on the term paper. Worse comes to worst, I'll hand in a piece of shit & take the final & hope I pass the course. I don't think that's the real worry on my mind, tho. It's more the void facing me until school starts in September, altho I'm not at all sure about *that* yet.

It's going to be especially difficult with Mrs. Ehrlich away - I've come to rely so much on her presence these past few months. I suppose that once I harness my will, I'll be fighting again, seeing people & doing things, sleeping well & feeling well. But until then, it's rough - & I don't feel I can *do* anything or go on with the business of living my life.

Tuesday, August 1, 1972

So with this page I begin the fourth year of my diary. It's 3 years since I first decided to keep a daily journal, & many changes have taken place. My life is now much more rewarding & fulfilling than it was in the summer of 1969 - filled with new accomplishments, new people, new outlooks. It's a good life, even tho it has its rough spots. I had one tonight.

Grandma Ethel was crying hysterically this evening, hurt because Jonny wouldn't eat the dinner she prepared & that he's "pushing her to go home." I guess she needs some sort of appreciation for her efforts. I couldn't bear it to watch her cry - but it's partially her own fault, altho Jonny *is* a spoiled brat.

But Mom & Dad have raised him the way they felt proper - I disagree, but he's not my kid & it's not my place. Eventually, I'm sure, the chickens will come home to roost & they'll have their hands full with Jonny.

In Classics this morning, we started *The Odyssey*. I loved reading the adventures of Odysseus - it's all so romantic & noble, altho a bit bloody near the end. I think Elspeth is going crazy: she said she dreamt last night that she married Jerry. I, on the other hand, dreamed that McGovern picked Liz Holtzman as his new running-mate. He'll probably opt for Larry O'Brien or a Catholic senator - the National Committee must meet to ratify his choice.

I had lunch with Scott, Stephen & Vito, who wants to drop his Speech courses. It's strange, but somehow nice, to be in a different crowd now than I was in the first summer session. Stanley dropped by LaGuardia this afternoon. He still spends most of his time seeing old movies, reading the Voice, the Times & the N.Y. Review of Books & dropping witticisms. What a waste. Stanley says he may come back in the fall, altho he's not certain as yet. He reported that Jay & Arthur are in Wash. State & have found jobs, & reminded me that Leon will be leaving for Wisconsin soon - I must call him. I also met Hesh today. He's one guy who'll never change - too bad, I say.

Monday, August 2, 1971

A sunny & cloudy day. When I got on campus this morning, I saw Timmy's unmistakable figure. He told me, after we had exchanged greetings, that he had left Scott & their friend Lewis in Los Angeles & arrived by jet at Kennedy at 1:30 AM. He told me, Emily & Fr. Regan about their cross-country adventures. The car broke down twice, they went hungry a lot, they were ripped into & they ripped off (with Timmy getting away with a federal rap for stealing steak at Yellowstone). They met a lot of freaks & people who hate hippies. It was interesting, but of course Timmy has a tendency to go on & on.

In Art, we saw sculpture by Rosso & the paintings & woodcuts of that weirdo, Edvard Munch. After class, I sat in front of LaGuardia with Timmy, Leon, Slade & Elspeth - we discussed baseball & stuff. Timmy drove me home & came in for a while, as he wanted Stacy's mailing address, to send her a card from Disneyland. Timmy has applied to SUNY at Purchase, but he doesn't think he can get in.

Shelli called - she had to stay home today because the REA man was coming to take her sister's things to Seattle. Jonny & I had to go to the dentist later in the afternoon. Dr. Hirsh filled a cavity of mine & gave Jonny a cleaning. Shelli came over after dinner from Kings Plaza - she wasn't surprised to learn that Timmy said Scott was fooling around with a lot of girls during the trip.

Shelli & I practiced tennis with Jonny, then went upstairs to bed. We had a bit of fun altho we didn't go all the way, as Shelli had her period. Shelli wants to go to Planned Parenthood soon, & I do, too.

Gary called - he's given up, or will shortly, his taxi driving job but he may get another in a liquor store. We got a card from Avis, who can't wait to get out of Norway. Grandma Ethel called - they're visiting Great-Grandma Bessie in the Catskills. Dad is having a lot of back trouble.

Sunday, August 3, 1969

I got up very late today - 10:30. It was too late to go to church. I went to Kings Highway to get the Village Voice. It seems there was real big gay power demonstration in Sheridan Square.

When I returned, Uncle Marty, Aunt Arlyne & Joey had come. The baby can now walk a little.

Brad called me and asked me if I wanted to have lunch with him. We ate at the Fillmore Queen (no remarks please!). We drove around for a while and played an interesting game: put "under the sheets" after the title of any song on the radio. It really works.

I like Brad. Do I love him? I don't think so. Not yet anyway. We discussed politics (he's still a Kennedy fan), music (he has a Simon & Garfunkel obsession), everything but sex. Why am I so inhibited?

Aunt Arlyne had a birthday party here.

Monday, August 4, 1975

7 PM. The heat wave ended today - it's still humid, but it was cloudy & not as hot as the weekend. I'm feeling pretty good, & a lot of the good feeling comes from yesterday. I'm glad that I decided to see Ronna & I hope our friendship will continue. Just her physical presence is comforting: that soft, chubby body is nice to have around. And at least I don't take her for granted this way.

I slept well & woke up early this morning to take the train into Manhattan. As I walked to the bus stop, I saw a cardinal resting on a branch. It's a magnificent red bird; I'd never seen one before, except in photographs. I also saw a magnificent sunflower as the Mill Basin bus passed Ocean Avenue.

We completed our translation of *Candide* in class today; Wednesday is our final, & on Friday we'll go over the test. I'm going to miss French class - Miss Belfer made it a very pleasant summer course.

On the train back to Brooklyn, a dog got on our car at

DeKalb Avenue. He was a cute little mutt & resisted all attempts to get him off the train. Everyone, especially the young people, was having a lot of fun with the animal. Finally, a transit worker with a walkie-talkie took charge, radioing for someone to meet him at the Prospect Park station with a rope. There were a lot of hoots, & the man said, "You think somebody having to get 28 rabies shots is a joke?" Still, the kids kept playing with the dog, & one Puerto Rican kid told another that the dog was his brother & then some guy shouted, "There's a lot of dogs on this train!" Anyway, at Prospect Park, the poor animal was coaxed off the train without having to resort to a rope.

At home, I did my exercises & had lunch. I called Cousin Michael, who was at home with a sitter while Robin was out; he's such a cute kid. I told him I'd come over for a visit one of these days. On Wednesday, Joel's taking him to the orthopedist again, & perhaps they'll put a boot on the cast so Michael can get around a little.

I went to the Brooklyn College library to do some work, but I ran into Elayne by the card catalog & we ended up going to the Sugar Bowl for coffee & a lime rickey. The Greek guys there asked Elayne if I was her brother.

She said that her job in the Art Dep't is in jeopardy because of the huge budget cuts, & odds are that she'll be fired in September. The whole fiscal crisis is causing so much personal suffering - I wonder if Josh will still have his job in the mail room when he returns. And Elayne threw a small scare into me when she said that some master's programs might be eliminated; I'm sure our small MFA program would be the first to go. I don't even want to think about that happening; I don't know what I'd do.

Elayne said she broke up with this vegetarian who she was seeing; she started telling me that he was a fantastic lover from the neck down but that he would never kiss her, & she couldn't take not being kissed while having sex. I don't know - is there some reason people tell *me* these intimate things, or is everybody into True Confessions these days? Elayne said, "It's all fodder for your pen"; that may be, but why does she have to mention these details at all?

She said she spoke to Elihu last evening & that he's back from his whirlwind trip & looking for students to tutor at LIU. Elihu did not see Leon in Madison - he went to Leon's house twice & no one answered the door altho Elihu thought he saw Leon behind a windowshade. Jerry & Shelli still live in that house with their friends. It seems Shelli persuaded Jerry to dye his hair orange & that it sticks up in the air 3 inches straight. And apparently Jerry's taken to cruising the streets of Madison at night; I don't know if he's hustling, but it sounds very weird. I feel sorry for Jerry & even more so for Shelli. When Elayne asked I was happy, I told her, "Just give me chocolate milk, cookies & a TV set or a book, & I'm content."

Monday, August 5, 1974

Listening to the news tonight, one is certain that Richard Nixon's days as President are numbered. Today, as he had to release very damaging tapes to the Congress & the courts, the President virtually admitted that he had played a role in the Watergate coverup. Senators of his party are asking him to resign, & many of the Republican congressmen who voted against impeachment on the Judiciary Committee will vote for impeachment in the full House. So the only question remains one of how Nixon will leave office: thru a curt resignation statement or a prolonged trial in the Senate ending in conviction. The momentum is unstoppable now; very often I've heard people use the cliché, "You're living through history," but it's really true now.

I had insomnia last night & didn't get to sleep until 5 AM. I suppose it's because I'm in the middle of a change in my life now. I'm virtually waiting for September & the start of the MFA program. I look at the want ads in the paper every day, but if I were serious about getting a job, I would have one by now. And I've done almost no work on my thesis; I probably won't finish it until the fall. I've got to get my life in some direction. I sometimes wonder if all my therapy has changed me into a different person or just made me a more comfortable, more successful neurotic.

I got a letter from Ronna today - she wrote about her adventures in Massachusetts, swimming, hiking, sightseeing. She said that even tho she misses me, she thinks the separation is good for her, giving her time to reevaluate things: "...after looking at all the pitfalls & things that are wrong with each of us separately & both of us together, I am still very happy with the relationship." And she writes about risk-taking: "The only way to overcome a fear is to plunge into it. It's not the physical risks but the emotional ones that are the hardest. Not commitments, not just leaving yourself open to being hurt, but to be given & to give emotions."

I needed people today & went out to see them. I dropped by the Courier-Life office to say hello to Mark, who was sitting at his desk with a picture of Consuelo & the baby on it. He was about to check on a story about a gangland killing in a Sheepshead Bay synagogue, but it was good to see Mark even if only for a little while. Three years ago was that awful dinner party at his house which ended with Shelli & me having a terrible fight; I wonder if Shelli told Mark & Consuelo all about that night & think I'm a terrible person. They haven't acted that way.

I drove out to Richmond College after lunch. I had missed that drive up Bay Street & the St. George area,

the college with its elevators & posters & crowds. I
waited in the lobby for Alice to drive her home. She
was surprised & extremely grateful; otherwise she
faced a 2-hour ride on the ferry, trains & bus. Alice
finally finished typing Marty's thesis but is now busy
with her class paper, due on Wednesday. A week
later, she's leaving for Europe. Alice's going to stay
with her brother in Stuttgart - I gave her Avis's
address in Bremen. Andreas came back from Geneva
on Saturday & so Alice understood my missing
Ronna, even after such a short period of time. Alice
said that everything's fine: Renee is complaining
about how depressed she is again. I dropped her off
at BC, where her bike was & lent her *Fear of Flying* &
said I'll see her before she leaves. Ronna's sister came
over to say hello to us; she was working in the
bookstore. She's angry they're not moving after all.

Thursday, August 6, 1970

Mansarde called last night - I'd been having Jonny tell
her I wasn't home, but I spoke to her last night. She
called, she said, to apologize for her behavior & to
thank me for my hospitality. I was cool to her - I don't
know where we'll go from here - perhaps nowhere.

This morning I took the train to Dad's place. Grandpa
Nat was glad to see me, & I did some work. They're
busy now, since Cousin Joel & Ben are on vacation.
Then Dad & I drove out to the Plainview warehouse.
The retail outlet started business today & did

smashing: $900. Uncle Marty was there, so were Norman & Harvey. We drove to nearby Huntington, where we had lunch at Cooky's, looked in on the Pants Set, & sold some goods to the man in Sid's store.

Our next stop was Green Acres, where we met Cousin Merryl in the parking lot. Rosemary had been crying when we came into the store - she's still terribly depressed & wants to go back into therapy. Dad took an order in Sid's store there while I shopped for certain items (stationery, film, Rolaids). It was tiring running around like that, but Dad seems used to it.

Tonight Marty & Arlyne picked up Mom & Dad - they had to go to a funeral chapel because Sid's mother-in-law died. Alice called tonight - she & Howie broke up after 17 months. I wasn't really surprised. They've been having problems for months. Alice tried pot recently & it doesn't do a thing for her. We got postcards from Jay from Calif. & the Grosses from Venice.

Thursday, August 7, 1969

I never got to sleep last night. I tried everything - hot bath, pills, TV, radio, reading. Nothing worked. I even tried masturbation. Hence, I'm exhausted.

I went to Kings Highway to buy the Voice & I saw Kjell there. I must call him.

Brad called me and asked me out to an early dinner. I was exhausted but I didn't want to miss the chance for company. We went to the Mill Basin Deli. Our waiter, St. Louis Blugerman Sheakespen, was a real nut - a taxi-driver, producer, director, author, playwright, poet, comedian & philosopher, he said. We had a lot of fun with him & he gave us his card.

Brad & I drove around & talked about sex. He says he's been with a different guy every night for the past 2 weeks. He says he's not promiscuous & wants me to act out my fantasies with him. He says that's the best way. I said I'd think on it & see him on his return.

Wednesday, August 8, 1973

6 PM. I've just turned off the TV. Vice-President Agnew, under possible indictment on kickback charges, denied any guilt. And tho Ronna & I watched the last of this summer's Ervin Committee hearings yesterday, that scandal is still very much in the public eye. As Mikey said to me last night, Speaker Albert may become the next President - what a mess!

As I predicted, I was awake until 3 AM, my mind clanking out ideas. God knows why these burst of creativity happen at such ridiculous hours, but who am I to argue with genius? Seriously, I know I am intelligent & creative, & even more than that, I know I can succeed in a variety of fields. I may go to law school next year or go on for a Ph.D. or possibly return to BC to go into their new Creative Writing MFA program - maybe I can do two of these things at once. I never have to worry about myself intellectually, only emotionally, & if I get things under control in that area, I feel I'm destined for great things. But I guess there is a price people pay: even poor Mike, running student gov't like a madman - Mikey said Mike's got stomach troubles again, & I'm sure it's due to pressure.

Still, I wrote some letters today: one to a soap opera actor, asking for an interview for one of those daytime TV fan magazines - I read about it in Writer's Digest - & another to Irna Phillips, creator of many soaps, asking for a job as an assistant writer. I have nothing to lose.

Ronna work me up this morning with exciting news: last night her mother got engaged to Harold. They'll be married in 6 months to a year, & Ronna said now she's got to file away all her doubts now that it's definite. Mrs. C went into the hospital today, but Ronna said she's so happy, she's floating on air.

Grandpa Herb & Grandma Ethel came over to go swimming in the pool today & I got another card from Gary, who seems to be having a ball in England. I'm glad for him & know he made the right decision - I bet it's really taken his mind off Hilda.

Monday, August 9, 1971

A hot, clear day. I woke up early & watched AM New York with guest host Robert Klein, whom Shelli idolizes. I kept trying to call him & ask him to stay away from her as a joke. I got a letter from Alice today. Altho she's probably back by now, I enjoyed the note - she wrote that she was having a ball, climbing the Alps, playing in the snows of the Matterhorn & seeing quaint out-of-the-way towns. I also got a letter from Avis, who enjoyed Copenhagen very much altho she's lost 10 lbs. & it's the porno capital of the world.

The Pontiac may not be ready for some time & I'm upset. I talked with Slade before class. He's initiated a policy of de-snobbification & even talked to Ronna this morning. In Art, we saw slides of cubist paintings by Braque & Gris. Rose was very upset because Marty had his draft physical today. He had notes from an allergist & a shrink - I hope he made out okay. After class, I talked with Laura, Avi & B.J. Laura's not really a bad sort, but she's kind of bland. Slade keeps saying how he wants to convince Laura & her boyfriend that he doesn't dislike them. Marv was on his way to do something for House Plan Association. He, too, wants to form a new party. As the fair-haired boy of the last election, he's going to sit on Bob's Academic Affairs Committee.

Shelli came along & we went home & had lunch. We

were kvetchy in my room, so we decided the best thing would be to go into the pool. It was beautiful in the water today - we played newcomb & badminton & read & kissed & slept. We had snacks afterward & then I had to take her home. Her jealousy of Fran is so funny.

Tonight I called Mikey. He & Mason are going to Boston for a few days. (Mikey's going to pick up Mason at camp) but wants to see me about having a Mugwump meeting soon to iron things out. I keep calling Gary, but no one has been home for the past three days.

Thursday, August 10, 1972

Life seems even more like a soap opera than ever these days. I never *could* get in touch with Debbie to make things definite about tonight. So, on the spur of the moment, Marc & I decided to go to the movies. We went to the Georgetowne to see "The Graduate." I enjoyed it, altho it seems a bit dated now. It was probably just my imagination, but as we were going out, in the dark, I thought I saw Jerry & a girl sitting down. I'm sure I'm wrong - but it did look like him.

In class this morning we finished "Oedipus," really a masterpiece. I hung around LaG for awhile, but Scott & Vito are getting on my nerves a bit, probably because I've been staying with them too much. I'm becoming certain that Barry's heading for trouble & I feel powerless to do anything.

I had a quiet lunch with Shira. She's a sweet person, very sincere. Hesh, she says, is getting used to seeing things like amputations & cardiac arrests - must be a messy business, tho. Back in LaG, I talked with Laura, Dick & Stanley, then went downtown to see Shelley Wouk. She & I had a good talk today, centering on my future.

We discussed whether I could be happy as an academician. Despite all my protestations, you know, I'm really half a Forsyte. That sense of property & possession is in me. Not like it's in Dad or Mom with their Cadillacs & jewelry, but it's there.

Gary called when I got home & I rushed over there. He only had come in for a few hours; he had to go to Peekskill for KP duty, so they took time off & came into B'klyn. Camp Drum was the usual shit, but Gary'll be leaving for Europe next week with a Reserve buddy. I took Gary to Kings Plaza, where the guys met for the trip to Peekskill, & I said I'd see him on Sunday or Monday. Being in the Guard is so shitty for him, I'm glad Gary's going to get away.

Speaking of getting away, I called Allan & the plans are set - he'll be leaving for Tampa at the end of the month, to live with his parents & go to school at U. of South Florida. Allan seems resigned to making the best of it, at least. I'll miss him, & I told him he can stay here when he comes up for Christmas.

Monday, August 11, 1969

I finished *City of Night*. It's a beautiful book. I found the ending scene with Jeremy very touching. Why *can't* dogs go to heaven?

I got the pictures back today - a few of them didn't come out. I don't know why photography interests me - maybe it's that moment frozen in time forever.

I saw "Goodbye Columbus" & thought it was very good. The theater was pretty crowded. The wedding scenes in the movie were so true to life. I think the message of the film is to decide for yourself what is right and what is not. But what if you're like Brenda Patimkin or me, and aren't sure?

I saw Caaron on the Mill Basin bus today. I wanted to talk to her, but I didn't have the nerve.

I'm trying to stay off the sleeping pills and just use the tranquilizers. I know now that I'm not going backwards. Excelsior!

Thursday, August 12, 1975

7 PM. I'm really tired & would like to go to bed early this evening, but I have company coming in an hour. I

invited Elihu over - we're both on such limited
bankrolls that we couldn't afford to do anything that
costs money. I'm too weary to play genial host &
exhaust myself trying to amuse him, so I'll just be my
usual discourteous self.

This was a hard day. I tried very hard to stay on the
Weight Watchers program & I only cheated at dinner,
when I had french fried potatoes as a side dish
(without ketchup, though). But it's a strain changing
my diet habits so drastically. I wonder if I'd rather
have a round tummy & be satisfied psychologically
than be, to use Alice's phrase, "slim & svelte" & be a
nervous wreck.

Our ebullient lecturer Iris possesses an ulcer - she
complained about it last night. She's funny but so
frenetic; I wonder if she's really happy even tho she's
attractive. I know the rate of recidivism at Weight
Watchers (& all diets) is very high; we saw examples
last night of "two-time losers," & I've seen in happen
among friends & acquaintances. The organization also
smacks of fanaticism (as do Alcoholics Anonymous,
Gamblers Anonymous & Synanon), which is
something I've never been able to put up with.

Of course these are all probably rationalizations. I
have to admit that I thought more about food today
than I have ever done in my whole life. I was starving
all through the night - my hunger was so bad that I
awoke at 5:30 AM, was unable to get back to sleep, &

so I had breakfast at 7 AM. All morning I thought of cupcakes, cookies & such. I did my exercises twice, I went out & bought some "legal" food. I went to the college to have my latest section of the novel xeroxed, then lay out by the pool even tho there was little sun.

Yesterday, while Gary was driving me home from St. John's, I spotted Stanley walking up Flatlands Avenue. Stanley stuck to the diet & he's slimmed down, but it still hasn't changed his life; he still leads an existence in limbo, measuring out his life with film screenings. Who am I to judge Stanley? But even so, being chubby has become part of me. Perhaps I'm afraid to become slim & more sensual & maybe that's why I'm not fat, either - I just stay on the outer edge of attractiveness. There are times when I wish I was in therapy again. Oh, who knows? Maybe inside every skinny person, there's a fat person struggling to come out.

Gisele came in to clean again today. Yesterday Gary & I pulled up as she was leaving, so she got a lift home with him. But today at 6 PM I drove Gisele home to Bed-Stuy. She's so concerned with my romantic life, always wanting to make sure I have a "wonderful" girlfriend & a potential mate. When I ask Gisele about herself, she just smiles & shrugs & says she doesn't want to try marriage again because she doesn't want the children to have a strange stepfather.

Libby phoned last night, trying to find if Teresa had a

car that she wanted driven to California. I told Libby
that I'd just heard from Teresa last week & she didn't
mention anything about it. I suggested she talk to
Costas or Melvin, who have spoken to Teresa more
recently. Libby told me she didn't want to bother
Melvin now, with his brother so ill. I asked about it &
heard the bad news: Melvin's and Milton's brother
Mendy collapsed on a biking tour. The diagnosis:
acute leukemia. Experimental drugs have put him in
what doctors call a "semi-stable" state, & now the
odds are 50-50 that the kid will live another 5 years.
What can one say or do when one hears things like
that? nothing, I guess. Mendy had just graduated
high school & was going to start college. Libby said
that Mason was in & that he's planning to do some
traveling after the summer. She said to come to the
Slope tonight, but I guess I won't be able to.

Thursday, August 13, 1970

A searingly hot day, as if the sun were trying to burn
all the evil out of this world. This morning I had an
auto accident downtown - nothing serious - the other
guy dented my rear fender. It was my fault, as I
wasn't looking. Mom did not get upset (Dad told her
it's only money) & neither did I.

I parked on Cadman Plaza & made my way past the
Hare Krishna chanters & walked into the State
Supreme Court Bldg. I couldn't stay long, as the meter
was only for 30 minutes. I saw one quick case in the

court of Justice Jones, a humorous black judge. It was a kidnapping case & the first time I've seen a man in handcuffs. A lot of retired old men who have nothing else to do attend these cases. I intend to go back. While I don't think I'll ever practice law, as of now I plan on going to law school.

After lunch, I went to the Marine to see "The Games," a surprisingly good movie about Olympic marathon runners - something that looks very exciting.

I felt enormously happy this evening, for no apparent reason. That's one of the best parts of being a manic-depressive. No one has "highs" like mine. Who needs marijuana? Today's mail brought a note from Cousins Bonnie & Alice & also the Ohio election code.

I spent the night on the porch with the family, the Bernsteins & Steven. Grandpa Herb came by to bring my slacks. Today was Mrs. Bernstein's birthday - she says Fern & Mark are in town.

Wednesday, August 14, 1974

Midnight. I feel content, but there are questions that trouble me. The foremost seems to be: Am I a child or a man, or am I condemned to live a life between those two stages? Last night I went downstairs & saw a whole pineapple in the refrigerator. I decided to cut it open so I could eat some slices & was about to begin when I heard Mom's footsteps coming downstairs. As old as I am, my heart still skips a beat & I feel enormously guilty (the way I did with the car on Monday).

I told her straight off, "I'm cutting open a pineapple." "I'll do it," she said & moved intently toward me. I moved away, she grabbed for the knife & I threatened her with it (while I was angry, I had no intention of hurting her, of course). She grabbed my arm & bit into it with her capped teeth. I shook her away & sliced the pineapple as she muttered about wanting me out of the house. Apparently she didn't see the contradiction in a 23-year-old being capable of living alone but not being able to slice a pineapple. No, I guess she knows that if she takes away my manhood in so many little ways (Today, when I took out the TV without asking her permission, she yelled, "Why did you disobey me?" Does she still think I'm 7 years old or will she forever be a parent & not a person?), she's got me where she wants me - in her control. Yet I realize my complicity in all of this: I am still living at home, after all, & I did allow her to bite my hand. In truth, it was a not unpleasant feeling. So here I am, sitting in a childish Oedipusville...

But tonight with Ronna, I was a man relating to a woman who loves me on an adult level. Ronna came over early this evening after an interview at her mother's office; she'll be working there next week. We went outside by the pool as the sun set red & powder blue, & we talked of books & linguistics & little things. Wendy called her today & spoke of Elton John & his manager, whom she loves, & inquired after Scott. Ronna's Uncle Abe, the brilliant doctor, has left his equally brilliant wife, Aunt Margie, for a young Asian med student in one of his classes. He's left their apartment & moved in with the girl into a Soho loft. Abe's the one at the seder who told Susan that Erica Jong "has gone commercial" - apparently he knows her.

I just enjoyed looking at Ronna. She's gotten a more mature look, a prettier face, since I've known her. I think that at 35 or so, she's going to be absolutely beautiful. We went to my room & watched TV. I enjoyed Carly Simon singing "That's the Way I've Always Heard It Should Be." All my friends from college *are* getting married now, soon to have children who'll hate them because of what they are not, & settling down to years of living on the debris of love. Everyone likes to think what they have is special & not like what anyone else has, but I'm aware enough to realize that Ronna & are not breaking any new ground with our relationship - but still, it's so good.

The laugh of the evening was when Fern knocked on the door & asked if I had a hole-puncher (for her brother Evan, who was downstairs); I leered Groucho-style & said, "Do *I* have a hole puncher?" We all laughed; I like my brother's girlfriend a lot. Then, left alone, Ronna & I made slow, steady love. I had missed her body, the roundness of her breasts, the whiteness of her belly, her underarm, navel & the hairs on the nape of her neck. It was a really fine sexual release for both of us. I feel so free with Ronna, free to be myself & to laugh & joke & be sad. The bed squeaked so, but we didn't much care. We talked & watched TV & read in bed afterwards, & I took her home a little while ago. With her, I feel I can really accomplish something in this world.

Wednesday, August 15, 1973

Altho Ronna probably hasn't even arrived in Cape Cod yet, I feel a kind of emptiness with her away. I suppose I've taken her for granted, but I realized today how much I love her. I miss her soft hair & cute smile & ironical brown eyes.

Last evening, when I went to pick Ronna up, her sister answered the door & it was obvious something was wrong. Ronna was sobbing audibly in her bedroom, & for a minute I thought she was upset because I keep pressuring her about being punctual. But her mother explained there had been a family fight & she'd left her favorite dinner (sausage) untouched - & I gathered it was about Harold. He was there, & for the first time, I liked him enormously last night; he's going to help me apply for a Fulbright (an idea that curiously came up earlier in the day's "burst of creativity") & he slyly mentioned that London is a lovely place for a honeymoon.

Ronna finally came out, apologized for being late, & coldly said goodbye to the others. She wore a yellow danskin top & a scarf, & altho she'd cleaned off her eyes, I could tell her mascara had been running. In the car, I told her if she didn't want to go to the movies, we didn't have to, but she said she would tell me about it before we got to Georgetowne. It was a minor fracas, involving Harold's "immaturity" & how he said that she couldn't break up him & her mother no matter what. Ronna said she can't live with them after they're married, so she'll apply to grad schools out of town.

We sat thru "Blume in Love," which I thoroughly enjoyed. Afterwards I held Ronna around the waist as we walked to my car as it was drizzling. She was hungry, so we went to the McDonald's in Rockaway near the Cross Bay Bridge & had burgers & cokes. She decided she'd straighten things out with her mother during the trip, & at her house, I hugged her tightly & wished her a good time. At home, I finished off a cute novel Ronna had recommended - it all took place on Staten Island (like my screenplay, if it ever does materialize).

Today I went to BC & found Mike & LeRoy & Stanley in the student gov't office. Mike is so busy. He's putting out a mailing, had lined up a Beach Boys concert & is trying for Albert Hammond too (Judy Rechman is his PR lady), trying to find a job for Mikey (altho Phyllis & Timmy will raise hell about

that) & placating Ethyle Wolfe, whom Dean
Birkenhead apparently stabbed in the back when he
cut School of Humanities funding in favor of Social
Sciences. Stanley was doing the film series & we
gossiped a bit. The last person to have news of Skip
was Elihu, who saw him at Sid & Elspeth's on the
Coast. I called Gary's father & found Gary will be
arriving Friday evening at Kennedy.

Monday, August 16, 1971

A cool, sunny day. Mom & Dad arrived last night
after 10 PM & they seemed to have enjoyed their
vacation. Last night President Nixon announced a
whole new economic policy to take care of inflation &
recession: a 90-day freeze on wages & prices, a 10%
import tax, an income tax cut, & a floating of the
dollar, which will virtually devalue it.

This morning I heard Dad talking to Mom over the
phone. He complained of chest pains & said the car
wouldn't be ready today - those Pontiac people keep
stalling & stalling. At school, I showed my sketches to
Elspeth, Leon, Robert & Al - they were not very
impressed, & I'm a bit discouraged. Avi brought some
old Kingsmans & it was hilarious going thru them &
seeing what our friends looked like two years ago.

In Art, Viola showed slides of paintings of Kandinsky
which I thought were shitty. After class, I ran into
Ray, who told me Mark helped Sue move. Ray wants

Elspeth's $60 share of the first month's rent, so I'm
supposed to tell her to call Sue.

I met with Avi about the first Spigot issue. I still
haven't done my story on the library yet. Harry came
by & startled me when he said that the new Student
Activities Director would be...Peter. Harry said he's
afraid the Student Assembly will be "reactionary" - &
that's coming from a conservative! I had lunch with
Baruch, who is such a nebbish.

When I got home, I saw Dad's car outside. He was ill
all day with severe chest pains. He's stubborn & won't
see a doctor - he never will. I hope it's not his heart. I
was upset & nervous all day because of it.

The Art paper is breathing down my neck. I've
changed the topic to the influence of comic books on
Lichtenstein's painting, & I only just started it. Shelli
spent the day with Avis, getting stoned & baking
cookies. There's a lot of pressure & things on my
mind now, & it's getting me down.

Thursday, August 17, 1972

In contrast to yesterday, by early evening today I was
feeling depressed. I still have to get thru 100 pages of
Plato's *Republic* & it's such dry stuff I can't bear it.
Perhaps it's because I have no discipline; that's
probably why I've been getting so fat lately. I've got to
lose weight desperately - I feel so fat that I can't go

out anymore. But the more anxious I get about it, the more I eat - it's a vicious cycle.

I got to sleep so late last night that I missed class today, & I'm really falling behind. I thought a lot about Stacy last night. She asked me if I was seeing anyone seriously, & I told her I was seeing lots of people comically. I know I could love Stacy, but it'll never work out - she has her world & friends & I have mine, & neither of us would give up anything for the other. We will never "get together," in her words, & maybe that's for the better. But I would like to sleep with her. Oh, I don't know, it's all such a comedy.

This morning Elspeth was wondering how to bail out some of her junkie friends who were arrested in L.A. for skinny-dipping. Sometimes I wonder if I'm not any better than old, whining, immature Elspeth. I sat around with Vito for the rest of the morning, talking about inconsequential stuff. At noon, we met Veronica & had lunch in McDonald's. Veronica's back from Europe & she'll be taking writing courses & being prose editor of Riverrun. I found out that she & Brian are first cousins - small world. Teresa joined us. I like her despite her rather flighty manner. She mentioned seeing "your old girlfriend & her husband" last night at Kings Plaza. "A despicable couple," she said.

I noticed Skip & John at another table & went over to say hello. They're both looking for work, & Skip said that Leon spoke to him last night, that he's found a place of his own, finally. Wisconsin, Skip reported, is a big beautiful school & Leon seems happy there.

I came home to on this cool, cloudy afternoon to try & get some work done, but so far I haven't succeeded. Scott wants me & Debbie to go with him & this girl to a Mets game on Sunday - I don't know yet. Dad has been on jury duty all week (he couldn't get out of it) & he's going out of his mind with boredom. I think the hotel is up for sale & the whole deal should be done soon.

Monday, August 18, 1969

As expected, I didn't get much sleep last night, but surprisingly, I'm not tired. I thought a lot about the play. I really feel like the character Donald, whose parents groomed him to be a failure & who can't understand why he prefers boys to girls & books to both & has anxiety attacks while driving on the Long Island Expressway.

I was so mad when I heard that Nixon appointed that idiot Clement Haynesworth to the Supreme Court. I'm not saying he should have appointed a Jew, but a judicial activist, a moderate if not a liberal. I'm disgusted with that imbecile in the White House & I called Sen. Javits' office to complain.

Today I didn't do much - went shopping, watched

TV, the usual garbage. Alice called. She & Howie went up to Woodstock but came back early, on Saturday. She thought I was high on something. We had a good, long friendly talk. I also had a nice talk with the Cohens & Mrs. Bernstein.

Tuesday, August 19, 1975

9 PM. The rest of the family is in the basement, entertaining Cousin Scott & Bobbi, who've come for a visit before they leave for Washington. Uncle Monty entered the hospital of Saturday - he was running 105 fever & the doctors have diagnosed it as pneumonia. Luckily (if I dare use that phrase), it's in the lung that collapsed; if it was in the other lung, it would be all over. He must know what Hell is. Aunt Sydelle says he hasn't eaten a thing in days & just was fading away even before the illness. I suppose the pneumonia was brought on by the chemotherapy weakening him. I'd visit him, but Aunt Sydelle told Dad he doesn't want to see people. Cousin Alice is coming up from Florida to stay with Sydelle. I don't know how long Monty has. It's a shame we're so cruel to the dying: we don't let them express their fears & their anger.

Today was a beautiful day, the kind of bright, mild weather we sometimes get around the middle of August following the dog days. I wrote & did research most of the day, so I was content. I feel so free when I can write; it's the most marvelous feeling. Now I'm interested in telling stories, which is one of the most important (& interesting) things to do in life.

On Friday Melvin & his brother Milton told me about a friend of LeRoy's, a brilliant guy, who got a 98 on his high school Regents; there was an essay question that said "Write a composition on your favorite place" & he started his essay, "My favorite place is the vagina..." & went on from there.

That's a great story, & so is the one Miss Belfer told about when she was an exchange student in France & she *tutoyed* (used the familiar) the director of the Institute & everyone sat around shocked, waiting for the distinguished old man to explode. Instead, he just patted her on the head & said, *"Petite Americaine."*

Alice understands about *people* being important. She showed me her story on Mr. Blumstein that just came out.

Last night I had a dream & this morning I wrote it up as a surreal story, for some reason using the third person & a character named August Billings. The dream started with Mikey telling me how he liked my body; he wasn't attracted to me sexually, of course - he just felt my body was comfortable & pleasant. I told him, quite honestly, that I felt the same way about his body, & then I proceeded to tell him a long story about Ronna, Susan, Felicia & Zsa Zsa Gabor letting gasoline out of the pumps of the crooked service station owner they all worked for. Then I was with Ronna: it was a Saturday night & we were walking up a street when suddenly she entered a shoe store & took an escalator upstairs. Everyone recognized Ronna for the film star that she was, but I couldn't catch up with her. It was like the Oscar Awards upstairs, & I tried to find Ronna, but a million girls looked like her & kept calling to me & a bunch of other guys. Then Ivan's mother, Mrs. T, said I could sit with her at her table in the back; she said she owed it to me. Mrs. T was Ronna's agent, & someone asked her how it felt to work for a big star like Ronna. I could only think about how I'd have to walk home alone & how that scared me. And that, basically, was what the story was.

I also wrote a one-page story based on my "*J'ai besoin du*..." dream. It's a trick story, one of those where a person wakes up from a dream only to find he's in someone else's dream, a bit of Bunuel & Borges there. Mom did not stop harassing me all day, & she's making it exceedingly difficult for me to keep to the diet. Still, I've got a fighting chance (underline that *fighting*). Poor woman, she's becoming permanently affixed with a scowl.

Thursday, August 20, 1970

A lousy, gloomy, rainy day. I woke up with stomach cramps & expected to have diarrhea, but I think I checked it with some medicine, at least for a while. There was a bright note - a letter from Gary. He's very happy with his on-the-job training as a file clerk, working in a pleasant air-conditioned office. But his "piece de resistance," as he termed it, was that he'll probably be coming home from Ft. Polk next Saturday, thus saving me the hassle of registering for him.

I drove to Korvette's on Bay Parkway & bought 2 hardcover books. One was The *Lord Won't Mind* by Gordon Merrick, a straight-forward novel of a lasting homosexual relationship. I think its candor upset me. I went to the Rugby to see "Bob & Carol & Ted & Alice," which I thought was a funny story of American morality today.

After supper, I had bad cramps again & naturally everybody left the house so there was no one to talk to. I'm very scared & I'm angry. Fear & anger seem to be quite characteristic of the neurotic boy. I say "boy" because I'm not a man yet - I'm too busy being scared & angry.

Just last night I was thinking that my stomach was fine for the past three weeks, but I just can't let things go right for very long.

Mel, the 86th St. manager, quit today. I got SMUT, the Young Mensa paper. I should write an article for it. Now I feel better.

Saturday, August 21, 1971

I spoke to Elspeth for a long time last night. She was very sympathetic, & when we hung up, I said, "I love you" - it just slipped out. I never thought of her as anything but a platonic friend - & I wouldn't have given it a second thought. I called Shelli when she got home from her date at 1 AM. She had a nice time, she said, but she thought of me all evening. We talked & I tried to hurt her because my ego was bruised. I felt better after we said we loved each other, but I still couldn't sleep at all.

I decided I'd go away to Rockaway for a few days to think thru & sort out my life again. But I first went to Shelli's house & we walked around the block. She said I was torturing her, that after all, I had urged her to date other guys. We took a drive out to the airport, thinking of seeing Elihu come home, but we decided we'd like to go to my house. And this afternoon was heaven - we discovered each other again. Mom, with a knowing smile, made us lunch, & then Shelli & I went into bedroom.

We had an afternoon of love, sexual & otherwise. She didn't really like Saul - just as a friend. He asked her out again Tuesday, & I told her to go, but she's undecided. We made love so many times I lost count - I'm exhausted. It was so damn beautiful, just like it used to be. When you come down to it, all you've got are trite clichés - like "we were meant for each other"

& stuff. I love her & she loves me & that's the way it's
going to be (I hope).

Driving around, we spotted Laura & her boyfriend
& went with them to Kings Plaza. We had dinner at
Bun 'n' Burger & walked around. In Macy's we visited
Li & I bought dungarees. Then we went to her house
& spent a quiet evening with her family. I spoke to
Gary & Shelli spoke to Elspeth. Elspeth told Shelli
what I'd said & wants to do "something nice" for me
tom'w. Shelli thinks Elspeth has a crush on me, but I
don't believe it.

Thursday, August 22, 1974

I spent yesterday in a blue funk. Talking the night
before, Mom said I was too "deep" & looked into
things too much, causing unhappiness. In the hospital
Grandma Sylvia told Cousin Robin the same thing.
But I don't think I'm particularly "deep," whatever
that means - I'm maybe more intelligent than most
people & maybe I perceive undertones others do not.
For a while on Tuesday night, stung by Dad's remarks
("Therapy hasn't helped you at all. You're lazy &
immature," etc.), I thought of going off somewhere &
locking myself in a Holiday Inn room (I have a credit
card there) & not telling anyone where I was for days.
That sounds so nice - only I would know where I was.
And I'd just think about my life & write & come to a
decision about whether to go on, & how to proceed,
living. In the face of questioning your whole

existence, so much of the pettiness in life seems meaningless - things like mixed marriage & political campaigns & fights over cleaning up. Am I a human being or merely a collection of symptoms?

The basic story behind Robin & Sandy (that's the black guy) is this: For quite a while, Robin didn't want her mother to phone or visit. So Aunt Sydelle figured something like this was up. She kept calling Joel at the place to pump him for information, but he didn't feel it was right to tell her his ex-wife's business. But then Michael said, "My mommy's going with a black man" (actually he's half-white) & Tuesday night there was a big confrontation at Robin's house, with screaming & pleading & threats & insults, & then Aunt Sydelle was frantic & told Monty to drive her here.

Mom called up Robin & tried to, as she said, "get the whole story." Mom feels that Robin's doing this merely to hurt Aunt Sydelle. That could be true, but isn't there the possibility of genuine love? Dad says that Robin's track record makes that unlikely. Anyway, from here on in, I'm an innocent bystander in this affair.

I felt better this morning after a night's sleep & a hundred pages of Philip Roth's latest novel, *My Life as a Man* - he's such a superb craftsman, always brilliant. I went to BC today. I've gotten my registration materials & I'm happily facing the reality of being in the MFA program. I register 2 weeks from tonight

& I can't wait.

I met Gary after encounters with the dumb but well-meaning Carol & the love-struck Li. We had lunch in Kosher King & I told him the trauma of Tuesday night. He's happy with the job at school but he still dislikes Columbia & he's getting closer with Kay. She was over at his house last night. We ran into Josh, whom I introduced to Gary. They talked, & it was funny to see two such diverse personalities interact.

Before I knew it, Ronna popped up. She had been told to work early, as things were very quiet. The four of us were talking about the difficulty of finding jobs when Stacy & Timmy approached from opposite directions. They passed us without saying hello although both of them knew each of us. They did half-heartedly wave to each other.

Josh & I went up to the English Dep't to try to find Baumbach, but we had no luck. After dropping Josh off, I went over to Ronna's. She was excited because her sister had gotten word that she'd passed her road test. We made very warm love lying sideways on her bed. The angle was so good, I really felt smooth & clean. We kept answering phone calls from her mother's boyfriends until finally Mrs. C came home & made us cheeseburgers for dinner. Ronna said at work she's been looking at that clock a lot lately, wanting time to move faster. It's probably because she doesn't like what she's doing.

Thursday, August 23, 1973

10 PM. Ronna's in the shower & I'm lying on top of
our double bed in our hotel room in Washington,
D.C. I'm really thrilled: today was a long day but very
rewarding. I woke up early, did my last-minute
chores & then went to Ronna's house to pick her up. I
was nervous about driving down the whole way, but
I never had a bad panicky anxiety attack. We stopped
after about 2 hours of driving - it was about noon - at
a Howard Johnson's on the Jersey side of the
Delaware Memorial Bridge. Ronna was so good to be
with on the drive down: she amused me & kept my
mind occupied.

We drove thru Delaware & Maryland - I got a bit
tired after we passed Baltimore, so we stopped again
& I had a coke & Ronna finished reading the letters
she got from Felicia & Susan. We were in Washington
by 3 PM, but it took us a long time to find the Gralyn
Hotel, where we had reservations (as Mr. & Mrs.
Grayson) - Washington traffic is confusing, but we
finally got to it.

The hotel's near DuPont Circle (I'd read about it in
Washington on $10 a Day), on an old-fashioned street.
It's a small, cheap place but it's quite pleasant; it was
once the Persian Embassy & you can still imagine the
luxuriousness of its past. The young man who owns it
or whatever (there's an old lady at the desk) took our
bags to our room, which is simple. We even got a

private bath at no extra cost. We rested for awhile. I
think Ronna's a little worried because we've never
shared a bed before, but I told her, "I didn't come to
D.C. just to get laid."

We went out for dinner at the Hot Shoppes Cafeteria
on Connecticut Avenue, where I had Thanksgiving
dinner with my family two years ago. Then we drove
over to Arlington & saw the Iwo Jima statue. From
there we went to the Jefferson Memorial. It's always
been my favorite spot in the city, & Ronna is a
Thomas Jefferson freak (they share the same
birthday). That statue of him, the simple beauty of the
monument, the fantastic view of the city all get to me.

The US Naval Band was to give a concert & people sat
on the steps. Ronna & I stayed there from sundown to
darkness, staring out over Tidal Basin. It was so
wonderful - we'd talked about going to Washington 6
months ago & we finally got here. Then we went to
see the Lincoln Memorial - that statue is very
awesome. I found my way back to the hotel with no
difficulty. Cat Stevens was singing "It's a Wild World"
on the radio as we passed Embassy Row.

Sunday, August 24, 1969

The night was not so terrible after all. I had a dream
that Tony, the guy down the block, was having an
asthma attack on Ave. T. Naturally I saved the day. I

spoke to Grandma Sylvia this morning, & everything seems fine.

Uncle Marty & Aunt Arlyne & the kids came over, along with Grandma Ethel & Grandpa Herb. Wendy looks very good but fat.

I got a call from Brad this afternoon. He called me a half-hour after he'd arrived home. He volunteered for first aid during hurricane Camille in Mississippi. He's leaving for Boston Tuesday for a friend's beachhouse & wants me to make some "wild, wacky plans" for next week. I think I've fallen in love with him, at least as much as I can fall in love with anybody.

I also called Gene, who is back from camp - he had a good time there. Maybe we'll get together sometime towards the middle of the week. Gary called too.

From Baldwin's *Another Country*: "The trouble with a secret life is that it's very frequently a secret from the person who lives it & not at all for the people he encounters."

Friday, August 25, 1972

I didn't get to sleep until very early in the morning. I was thinking about things - Allan's moving to Fla. is bound to change things at school. Leon is gone, & so are Charles & Elayne, & Gary will leave shortly. And then, so will I - no more LaGuardia lobby to hang around in. Well, that's life.

I like Skip, but I don't think he likes me very much altho he's nice to me. But it was okay just to sit in his funny, dirty ap't with those cats, playing scrabble with him & Allan, who had been to the Kinks concert with Fat Ronnie, who's a good friend of Ray Davies. Allan said he'd bumped into Elspeth there & couldn't get over how well she'd looked: "pretty," Allan said.

I awoke much too late to catch my class - I got on campus at noon & met Vito & Nina, who had just come from OTB to bet on some horse race. Vito & I drove over to Veronica's house in Sunset Park, as he had need of one of her stories to use in a speech to entertain. Driving over, Vito told me that this morning he was in his grandmother's house & a good-looking young man came to deliver slipcovers. They talked & the slipcover man kissed Vito.

Veronica's parents were so nice: her father shook my hand & then said to his wife, "Handsome boy, that Richie." (I later learned he does that with everyone.) We got rid of Veronica's twin sister & her boyfriend Junior, who were just getting out of bed - together, apparently - & then Veronica & Vito & I sat around the kitchen talking. Her stories are kind of Donald Barthelme-ish, weird but very cute. Veronica's a very clever person, one of those people who have absolutely no interest in sex or material possessions.

We left, & after I dropped Vito off on Coney Island Ave., I came home to find, incredibly, that the pool had collapsed. What a fucking mess.

I got a letter from Vogue Magazine - Elihu's handwriting - & one from Avis. She wrote, "I love you very much, I miss you very much...I'm looking forward to our long talks over Coke & French fries at Campus Corner." She asks if I could pick her & Libby up at Port Authority on Monday. Of course I'll do it. Avis said that even if I want to get involved with Stacy, she'll still be my friend. What a good friend Avis is. Those words - "I love you very much" - meant more to me than any words I've received in a letter in years. I love you too, Avis.

Wednesday, August 26, 1970

A bright-hot Women's Liberation Day. I went to City Hall & there were over 1,000 people for a rally before the march. I posed as a press photographer & took photos of Betty Friedan, Ellie Guggenheimer & Bella Abzug. Miss Friedan, a leader in Women's Lib, talked to dozens of reporters. The press had a field day.

Their demands are reasonable - day-care centers, ending job discrimination, free abortions - but some of the far-out girls turn me off. The "male chauvinists" in the crowd seemed to be more amused than outraged. I like girls to be feminine, but perhaps because of my own hangups I view them first as people, only second as women.

Dad took the day off, & he & Mom went to Kings Plaza, which is going great guns & should be ready to open soon. Gisele came in to do the housework for today. The Bernsteins came over this afternoon & asked me to get a jacket their son left at the Feingolds' house. Mrs. F said she was against today's "nonsense" & so were Mom & Mrs. B.

Uncle Marty went with his friend Pogo Joe Caldwell to a basketball clinic upstate, & Dad's quite annoyed with him for taking so many days off. He's not even attending to his own Slack Bar business, & Grandpa Herb has to work every day since Marty's on vacation. Ben came over tonight while the family was out to bring a $2000 check to Dad.

Gary's mother called & said I could come with them to the airport Saturday night. George Cincotta's running for boro president - he's a sad little man. We called Las Vegas - Dr. H is having complications & won't be able to leave the hospital as soon as planned.

Tuesday, August 27, 1975

5 PM on an absolutely magnificent day: warm temperatures, lots of sunshine & low humidities (so that my stuffed-up head of yesterday has finally cleared up). Reading Maslow's book is exciting for me, because I find that I have a lot in common with

his self-actualizing subjects. I understand what he means by "peak experiences" because I have had them: last year at the BC graduation & Phi Beta Kappa installation & my birthday in June, & then again in November on the day I drove to Hempstead Lake Park (the day inspired my story "The Smile in the Closet"); early Xmas morning, after Hoops' dismal get-together; & last June, after Libby's party.

But I've felt it - the almost unbearable feelings of unity, wholeness & goodness - to a lesser degree on other occasions: after dates with Ronna; after teaching a good lesson at LIU; & after writing something I consider to be worthwhile. Never, six years ago, did I ever think there could be moments like those; and those moments, as brief & fleeting as they are, make life worth living. I have a completely different attitude toward life when I feel like that: there is zest & joy & delight & very little fear or anxiety. Life just seems to be getting richer & richer.

I spoke to Ronna last night, & she told me about the wedding on Sunday & how nice it was; I'm sure she made a beautiful bridesmaid. She said she felt somewhat let down afterwards, which is understandable. Ronna was also saying goodbye, for she & her family were leaving for a week on Cape Cod today. She was intending to take a bus back next Saturday because she had promised Susan weeks ago that she'd go with her to see "Daisy Miller" & the film would be coming to the Carnegie Hall Cinema this weekend (for one day only); of course Susan was holding Ronna to her promise.

Ronna was kind of upset about it, & her mother thought she was being stupid to come back. I couldn't help putting my two cents in & I told Ronna, "Of course, you know I'd advise selfishness..." No one but Ronna would interrupt a lovely vacation to see a movie (a bad one, no less) with Susan. I think my words had some effect on her - I told her to imagine how she would feel on that bus trip back - for she said was going to call Susan & try to get out of it.

I like being Ronna's friend, & I told her that when she gets back to the city, we should get together one day. I felt so good after our conversation.

Dad called Aunt Sydelle last evening (he's been putting it off because he dreaded it so) & there was bad news: the doctors aren't sure Uncle Monty will get out of the hospital this time. They've been trying to treat the pneumonia, but he's been running a high fever for 10 days & he's just deteriorating. Monty knows the nature of his illness, but still he harbors hope for a recovery - that's human nature. But his nephew the doctor told Sydelle that nothing can be done except to make him as comfortable as possible. At least he's not in much pain.

I ran into Mark & his family this afternoon: all 3 and 1/2 of them, for Consuelo looked slightly bigger & she informed me that Miguel will have a brother or sister next January. Mark has been laid off for 7 months & hasn't been able to find a job, so he figured he might as well return to Brooklyn College & get his B.A. finally; he'll be taking a couple of evening courses in the fall.

It's so strange how things work out in time. Mark told Miguel, "This is Richie, but not the Richie you're used to." He meant Richie C, of course. There was some news: Shelli's parents have moved; & Don is in San Francisco, where he passed the California bar exam; & Mark & Consuelo have become friendly with Ken & his wife. Consuelo is hoping to get a job as a Bilingual teacher soon, & they both look well. It was good to see them & I hope to keep in touch with them.

I saw Melvin & Mavis on the quadrangle grass, & also Harry & his wife & Elayne were around, & so were Deans McGee & Jones. So summer is over and another school year at BC - my sixth - is beginning.

Saturday, August 28, 1971

The hurricane swiftly & furiously passed through the city during the night. I slept through it all, but this morning there were uprooted trees & the pool was overflowing. Yet the sky was a remarkably clear powder blue. Perhaps the storm washed away the smog & pollution. I had a long night's sleep, but I felt very tired this morning.

Shelli called me & we decided I'd pick her up at noon. Wendy called Shelli last night & told her about her date with a guy she'd picked up at Wetson's. It seems Phyllis told Carol that Shelli hated her - big deal. This morning I did some reading & then went to Shelli's house. She looked more beautiful than usual as she waited for me outside.

We drove into Prospect Park & I bought her a balloon at the zoo. We went on this surrey-trolley kind of ride around the park & it really made me carsick. Shelli was dizzy too. We drove to my house, where I found a letter from Stockholm, from Jerry.

He seems blissfully happy, living in Sweden with the family of Borje - "the finest friend I have ever had." He booked passage on a boat leaving tomorrow for Britain. Borje is now seeking to avoid Allan "after a disastrous incident in Munich," which Jerry doesn't elaborate on. He also told me to "stop throwing away money on that half-wit shrink."

I called Elihu & asked him if I should tell Jerry's parents about his whereabouts: maybe he doesn't want to know about Mrs. H's condition & maybe she's improving. Elihu was unsure. He looked up in a book when Jerry's boat would be arriving. I'll call Elspeth next.

Shelli & I had a luncheon on the grass - I had gotten

stuff from the deli - & then we went upstairs & had a delicious time. She was in pain when I first entered her vagina, so perhaps she's getting her period. I hope so. I couldn't take another month like last one. But we're going to Planned Parenthood this week.

We bought birthday cards for Slade & a huge polyethylene snake for him. Tonight I did my Art work & spoke to Gary, who was at the Armory on Guard duty all day.

Thursday, August 29, 1974

Tonight I've got my journalistic cap on. At times it's good for me to stop my self-analysis & probing & instead concentrate on being an observer of the human condition. When I was little, I always wanted to be, not the leading characters in movies or TV shows, but the supporting characters, those to whom nothing happened, the ones who merely commented on the protagonists' situations - the whole "I Am a Camera" bit.

Last night I picked up Ronna after the thunderstorm abated. She looked pretty & fresh. Her sister was going out with last year's boyfriend Harris, or Hank - she told Ronna that he's changed & he kisses better now. Ronna also told me a secret: that Felicia's brother (he of the streaking & the tattoo) propositioned her sister, who was impressed when he told her he's become a hedonist. Ronna says that her sister's really happy having lost weight, & Ronna wants to drop some pounds too.

I drove Ronna to this house to pick up something for her mother; then we went on to the Heights, to walk along Montague St. We straightened a lot out: Ronna *did* say that I make it difficult for her to tell me when she's angry, which is what I figured. And she's jealous of my financial position & my lack of responsibility in that area, something I can readily understand.

We came back to my house to watch the news & chat. I mentioned seeing Howie from the window of the 42nd St. bus last week, & Ronna said that he's become very nervous. He & his girlfriend are moving in together, altho Felicia says that the girl would like to leave Howie but is afraid he'd kill himself if she did - all of which may be wishful thinking on Felicia's part. Susan's novel is complete & I'd like to read it. I hear I'm satirized in it - shades of Lawrence & Huxley!

Ronna & I found the announcement of the birth of Dad's partner Lennie's sister's child; the sister's married to a Monticello trotters rider, & the announcement was so stupid, saying "New Foal: Jennifer Mara; Mare: Karen; Stallion: Jorge." But that whole family is crazy.

After taking Ronna home, I lay awake thinking. I had a crazy thought about Jerry's marrying Shelli & then being gay: maybe he went out with Shelli as a way of

getting sexually close to me, maybe he liked me &
was too repressed at the time to go to me directly -
not that I was ever attracted to him, as he's not my
type. Anyway, could that be a reason for his hatred of
me? No, it was an off-the-wall idea.

This afternoon I was lying on the beach at Rockaway
right by the water, reading Doris Lessing. Lee passed
with 2 friends - he came over & shook hands (I almost
made a faux pas & shook 'regular' instead of 'cool-
soul-hip'; it's such a problem these days). Lee was
working at a camp this summer & goes back to
Hofstra Law soon. He asked if I see the Kingsman
crowd, & I said, "Mostly just Ronna" - he said he sees
Hal & Laura & heard from Lewis & Li. I almost didn't
recognize Lee, as it's been years since I've seen him
without a beard or mustache.

After Lee left, just a few minutes later, Peter came by
in the opposite direction. This time I shook hands
right, & he sat down. He got back this morning from
the Canadian Rockies & said it was beautiful. He's
been studying dance this summer with June Lewis - I
nodded, having vaguely heard of the name - & he's
managing the AYH (American Youth Hostel) store, a
job he'll probably give up. Peter said his brother's still
away in the White Mountains, & that he, Peter, is
thinking of subletting the Bethune St. Village ap't of
some lady dancer. He had to rush off to take his ailing
dog to the vet.

Thursday, August 30, 1973

I didn't get to sleep until late last night, thinking about people. I decided why Leon takes people to his bosom & then suddenly drops them; it's happened with Harvey, the Klayman brothers, Corey & now Skip. He can't let people get too close to him, & when they do, he uses some excuse not to speak with them. Very sad. And while I don't see how Skip could do such a thing as literally prostitute himself, it's not really doing anyone any harm, except maybe Skip himself. Why should I judge others? Yet I find myself doing it & I detest myself for it.

I spoke to Ronna early this morning, very briefly, as she was rushing to get her brother to his psychiatrist on time. She told me she doesn't think she'll be seeing Carl anymore & then had to go before she could explain fully. I decided to meet her at Billy's doctor's office (she had said she wanted to see me later) & so I stood outside the building on Plaza St. & surprised them when they came out.

We went back to Ronna's house & she made us lunch; then she & Billy changed into their bathing suits & came to our pool. Billy really loved the water; the kid went on the raft & played ball with me & Ronna & Jonny. It was another near-100-degree day & it was impossible to sit outside without swimming.

While Mom was giving Billy something to eat, Ronna

told me about me about last night. She made Carl dinner, & then, in Billy's bedroom, told him about me. He said that he was seeing a girl, too (altho Ronna didn't quite believe him) & said he wanted to take her to the movies anyway. Just before they got to Kings Plaza, Ronna felt guilty & Carl got angry - "just the way Ivan did," she said. (Apparently I get angry in a somewhat different way.) Finally they do go in to the theater. At the end of the evening, he told her, "Thanks anyway," so she doesn't think she'll be hearing from him anymore. I feel more sorry for Carl than relieved for myself. I even got the idea of fixing him up with Avis when she gets back (soon, I hope - I miss her), but that's rather absurd.

Ronna & I took her brother back to their house, along with the kissing Guarami fish that Marc gave Billy (Marc wanted to get rid of it & all Billy's fish had died). Ronna's sister came home, so Ronna & I were free to have dinner at the Charcoal Chef in Canarsie. It was a pleasant meal, & when I took her home, I came up for awhile. Harold wasn't feeling well & went home by bus; he wouldn't let Ronna's mother or me drive him home. Mrs. C seemed mystified by his behavior. I kissed Ronna goodnight - we've become very domestic since our trip to Washington.

Thursday, August 31, 1972

It was good to enter the world once again. Last night Avis called to ask if she & Ike could come over. I felt okay, so I said sure. And after that, I got a call from Alice, who said she'd come over, too. They arrived at the same time: Alice on her trusty bike; Ike determinedly hobbling up the stairs; & Avis looking as beautiful as ever. We sat in the living room & talked; Avis & Ike told about their summer at camp. Ike is a very amiable, open person & I can't help liking him. Alice is taking over as manager of Vanderveer for awhile. She said Renee's annulment hearing is today. Renee had asked her to testify to the fact that David had promised to buy her a house & then reneged, but Alice wouldn't do it. Everyone got on very well - a successful evening, I think.

This morning, as I returned to the campus, I found it swarming with freshmen, in for orientation. I was even mistaken for one - imagine, a man of my position! Classics was short today - tom'w is our final & I've been studying hard. I ran into Debbie with some of her hitter friends, & she said she'd call. Vito told me he'd spotted the slipcover man on campus - but when Vito approached the guy, he said he wasn't the same person. Vito is sure it was.

In SUBO, Club fair was in progress. I helped Peggy man the Classics Club table, & I walked around to see people. Melvin said he & Timmy had a good time, but they nearly got busted in Tel Aviv for drugs. Pat, the new ACA president, was coordinating things; Skip, John & the other Gay People were serving fruit salad; Sid was getting people for Young Democrats - he caught my cold. Harry, Hesh, Ira, & George were there for APO; Bernie for Spigot; & Ronna & Maddy at the Kingsman table.

I went to LaG & chatted with the deans, then had to go to the bookstore, where I met Mikey, who'd just cycled in from Rockaway. He said that he, Josh, John & Skip had a nice farewell dinner with Allan in Chinatown. Also, he'd heard from Leon, who's okay & playing stickball in Madison. After wishing Hal a good year at Rochester, I came home to study.

Monday, September 1, 1969

Today was Labor Day - the first day of September - the psychological end of summer. I awoke groggily after a drug-induced sleep which was wracked with dreams. It was hot & smotheringly humid today. I went to the Junction, got on the Seventh Avenue express to Atlantic Avenue & came back home on the D train. The new exact fare system on the buses is a drag, but I suppose it will reduce holdups of drivers.

Aunt Sydelle, Uncle Monty, Scott & the twins came over at about 2 PM. We really had a lot of fun at the pool, playing a sort of war, with the boys on one side & Bonnie & Alice & me on the other. Kid stuff, but fun. I can now tell the twins apart - Bonnie's taller. We had delicatessen for lunch. I really surprised myself by having a good time.

I'm now trying to relax on the eve of my third road test with a steaming glass of Keemun tea with rosefruit added. I hope the rest of the month & the rest of the fall is this good.

www.ingramcontent.com/pod-product-compliance
Lightning Source LLC
Chambersburg PA
CBHW022108280326
41933CB00007B/298